The Vacation Rental Organizer

Christine Hrib Karpinski

Published by Kinney Pollack Press
www.HowToRentByOwner.com

ISBN: 978–0–9748249–1–8

Printed in the United States of America

How to use this Book

The Vacation Rental Organizer is specially designed to help you track and organize your vacation rental business. Most of the pages in this book are self-explanatory, just fill in the appropriate fields and you are good to go.

The date pages can be used for either nightly or weekly bookings. First, determine how most of your bookings will be reserved, then set your date pages up accordingly — either nightly or weekly (see examples).

For weekly rentals, decide whether you are going to rent Friday to Friday, Saturday to Saturday, etc. Notice the two-page spread has eight columns, one column for each corresponding day (one weekly rental spans seven nights but eight days. Typically you will have one renter depart and another arrive on the same day). In the example below, I have written the dates July 24-31 across the top of each column. The Jones's have booked this full week, for arrival on Saturday, July 24 and departure on Saturday, July 31. Setting up your book this way, rather than the typical seven-day calendar for Sunday to Saturday, will allow you to view one weekly rental period without having to turn pages. This also makes it easier for you to quote your renters the dates of arrival and departure, thus avoiding confusion and the possibility of double booking your property.

For nightly rentals however, you will only fill the dates into seven columns. In the example, I have left the first column blank and filled in the dates for Sunday July 25 through Saturday, July 31. In this example, The Jones family will arrive on Sunday, July 25th and depart the morning of Tuesday, July 27th. The Clark Family will arrive on Tuesday, July 27th and depart on Friday, July 30th. The Davis Family will arrive on Friday, July 30th and depart on Saturday, July 31st.

For both weekly and nightly rentals, be sure to fill in all the information in the field that corresponds with the name at the top of that day/week.

In your organizer, you will want to keep track of all inquiries and bookings you get from renters. Develop a system of jotting down notes about each person you speak with so that you can refer back to who they are when you have further conversations (either email or phone). Don't forget to keep track of where the renters found you. When it comes to portal renewal time (payment due to the listing sites), you will want to know how many

Date *July 24*

DATE *July 24*	DATE *July 24*	DATE *July 24*	DATE *July 24*
Renter Information			
Name	*Smith*	*Smith*	*Smith*
Address	*1234 Home Street*		
City, State, Zip	*Atlanta, GA*		
Telephone	*30004*		
E-Mail	*404-404-4040*		
# of Nights	*Smith@AOL.com*		
____ Adults ____ Children	*7*		
# of Vehicles	*4/4*		
Tag #	*/*		
Pets	*GA CDE123*		
Referral Site	*None*		
Date Reserved	*How to Rent by*		
Rate	*Owner*		
Fees	*February 1*		
Taxes	*$1,000/wk*		
Check List	*$75 cleaning*		
Sent Billing Agreement ☐	☑	☐	☐
Rental Rules ☐	☐	☐	☐
Directions ☐	☑	☐	☐
Deposit Returned ☐	☐	☐	☐
Rec. Deposit & Signed Rules ☐	☐	☐	☐
1st Payment ☐	☑	☐	☐
2nd Payment ☐	☐	☐	☐
Scheduled Cleaning ☐	☑	☐	☐
Cleaning Feedback ☐	☐	☐	☐
WEEKLY TOTALS *$1,182.50*	**NIGHTLY TOTALS** *$1,182.50*	**NIGHTLY TOTALS**	**NIGHTLY TOTALS**
RENT *$1,000.00*	**RENT** *$1,000.00*	**RENT**	**RENT**
TAXES *$107.50*	**TAXES** *$107.50*	**TAXES**	**TAXES**
CLEANING FEES *$75.00*	**CLEANING FEES** *$75.00*	**CLEANING FEES**	**CLEANING FEES**

HowToRentByOwner.Com

Date *July 31*

DATE *July 24*	DATE *July 24*	DATE *July 24*	DATE *July 24*
Smith	*Smith*	*Smith*	*Smith*
☐	☐	☐	☐
☐	☐	☐	☐
☐	☐	☐	☐
☐	☐	☐	☐
☐	☐	☐	☐
☐	☐	☐	☐
☐	☐	☐	☐
☐	☐	☐	☐
☐	☐	☐	☐
NIGHTLY TOTALS	**NIGHTLY TOTALS**	**NIGHTLY TOTALS**	**NIGHTLY TOTALS**
RENT	**RENT**	**RENT**	**RENT**
TAXES	**TAXES**	**TAXES**	**TAXES**
CLEANING FEES	**CLEANING FEES**	**CLEANING FEES**	**CLEANING FEES**

HowToRentByOwner.Com

(Example: Weekly)

qualified inquiries came from that site. By qualified, I mean how many inquiries actually resulted in a booking. Don't just count your emails. From one of my listing sites, I got 30–40 rental inquiries a week, but I never had one booking, so I did not renew my membership to that site. In other words, make sure you are getting enough bang for your buck.

Another thing you should make a habit of is photocopying each check you receive from renters. If you do not have a copier at home, most banks will photocopy them for free when you are depositing. Take that copy of the check and staple it right on the corresponding page for that booking. This will make it very easy to see if you have received a payment or not, as well as give you all the renter's information (name, address, etc.) from his or her check. Also, this is a good practice for income tax purposes. At year-end, or God forbid during an audit, you will have all the information available at your fingertips.

As for signed and returned rental rules and payment agreements, no need to staple these into your rental book. They will make your book too bulky. Just file them away. The only time you will need these is if you have problem renters, which (thankfully) is not often. If you do have a problem renter, and you have to keep a portion of the security deposit, then you'll want to staple that correspondence into this book.

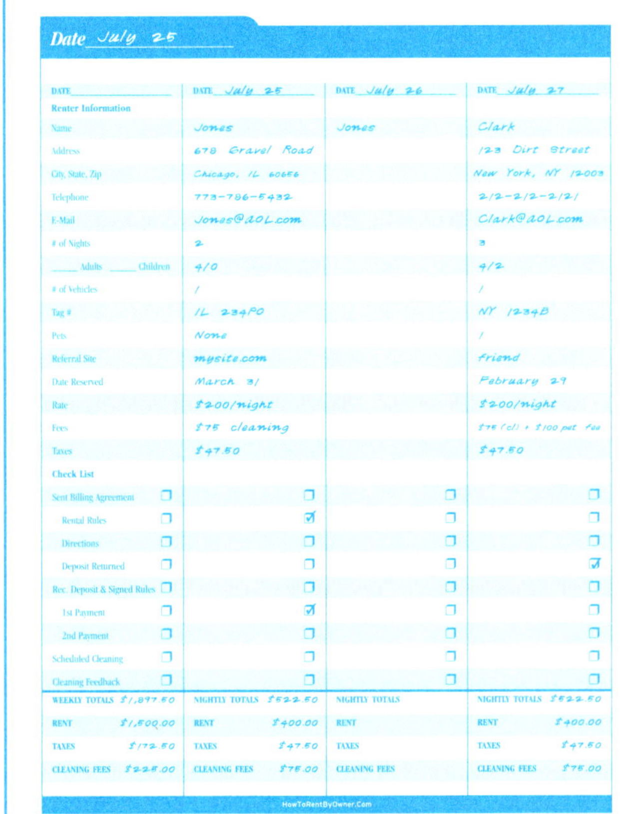

Date July 25

DATE ____	DATE July 25	DATE July 26	DATE July 27
Renter Information			
Name	Jones	Jones	Clark
Address	678 Gravel Road		123 Dirt Street
City, State, Zip	Chicago, IL 60656		New York, NY 12003
Telephone	773-786-5432		212-212-2121
E-Mail	Jones@aOL.com		Clark@aOL.com
# of Nights	2		3
____ Adults ____ Children	4/0		4/2
# of Vehicles	1		1
Tag #	IL 234PO		NY 1234B
Pets	None		1
Referral Site	mysite.com		friend
Date Reserved	March 31		February 29
Rate	$200/night		$200/night
Fees	$75 cleaning		$75 (cl) + $100 pet fee
Taxes	$47.50		$47.50
Check List			
Sent Billing Agreement ☐	☐	☐	☐
Rental Rules ☐	☑	☐	☐
Directions ☐	☐	☐	☐
Deposit Returned ☐	☐	☐	☑
Rec. Deposit & Signed Rules ☐	☐	☐	☐
1st Payment ☐	☑	☐	☐
2nd Payment ☐	☐	☐	☐
Scheduled Cleaning ☐	☐	☐	☐
Cleaning Feedback ☐	☐	☐	☐
WEEKLY TOTALS $1,897.50	**NIGHTLY TOTALS** $522.50	**NIGHTLY TOTALS**	**NIGHTLY TOTALS** $522.50
RENT $1,500.00	**RENT** $400.00	**RENT**	**RENT** $400.00
TAXES $172.50	**TAXES** $47.50	**TAXES**	**TAXES** $47.50
CLEANING FEES $225.00	**CLEANING FEES** $75.00	**CLEANING FEES**	**CLEANING FEES** $75.00

HowToRentByOwner.Com

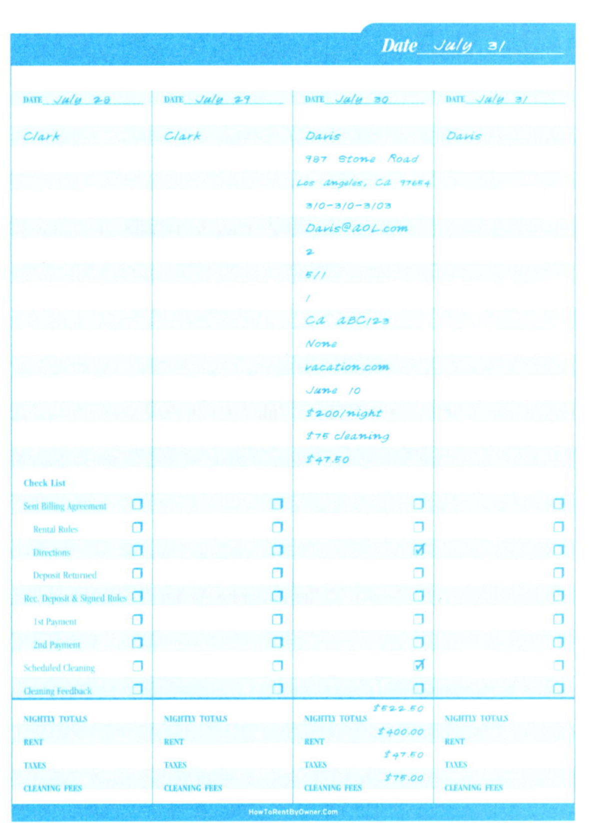

Date July 31

DATE July 28	DATE July 29	DATE July 30	DATE July 31
Clark	Clark	Davis	Davis
		987 Stone Road	
		Los Angeles, Ca 97654	
		310-310-3103	
		Davis@aOL.com	
		2	
		5/1	
		1	
		Ca ABC123	
		None	
		vacation.com	
		June 10	
		$200/night	
		$75 cleaning	
		$47.50	
Check List			
Sent Billing Agreement ☐	☐	☐	☐
Rental Rules ☐	☐	☐	☐
Directions ☐	☐	☑	☐
Deposit Returned ☐	☐	☐	☐
Rec. Deposit & Signed Rules ☐	☐	☐	☐
1st Payment ☐	☐	☐	☐
2nd Payment ☐	☐	☐	☐
Scheduled Cleaning ☐	☐	☑	☐
Cleaning Feedback ☐	☐	☐	☐
NIGHTLY TOTALS	**NIGHTLY TOTALS**	**NIGHTLY TOTALS** $522.50	**NIGHTLY TOTALS**
RENT	**RENT**	**RENT** $400.00	**RENT**
TAXES	**TAXES**	**TAXES** $47.50	**TAXES**
CLEANING FEES	**CLEANING FEES**	**CLEANING FEES** $75.00	**CLEANING FEES**

HowToRentByOwner.Com

(Example: Nightly)

You will also want to keep good track of the various services you pay for. Keeping up with the maid's payments, lawn maintenance, and other weekly or per-rental maintenance bills can easily get confusing (it's happened to me), especially if you are working with an individual who does not have a formal billing system established. Be sure to write in your book the check number that you paid with and it's corresponding billing date.

You will also want to write down the make, model and serial number of major appliances. This is critical information to have on hand if you ever need to call a repairman. Also, keep tract of all the service you have done.

Another major advantage of keeping all this information in a book is when you go to sell your property, you can easily show the buyer the past records proving your rental history and maintenance records. Now you're selling an established business rather than just another property.

By now, I think you can see the importance of organization. Your vacation rental business will never work if you have little scraps of paper with scribbling scrawled across them. No, that's for your kid's lemonade stand. This is serious business. I am confident that you will find *The Vacation Rental Organizer* an invaluable resource for organizing your vacation rental business.

Happy Renting!
Christine

Property Information

Property Name Can't Bear to Leave

Complex Name

Address 2464 Hackberry

City, State, Zip Sevierville Tn 37862 Unit #

Web Site Address

Lock Box Code Date

Home Owners Association (HOA)

Contact Person Cindy Hannah

Address

City, State, Zip

Telephone 704 641-5761

Email cindyhannah06@Gmail.com

Web Site Address

Notes:

Mortgage Information

1st Mortgage Bank/Lending Instituiton

Company

Account #

Interest Rate | Payment Amount

Payment Address

City, State, Zip

Web Site Address

Equity Line

Company

Account #

Interest Rate | Payment Amount

Payment Address

City, State, Zip

Web Site Address

Company

Account #

Interest Rate | Payment Amount

Payment Address

City, State, Zip

Web Site Address

Company Burns Ins + Williams

Account # Joe Burns

Interest Rate | Payment Amount

Payment Address

City, State, Zip

Web Site Address

Company

Account #

Interest Rate | Payment Amount

Payment Address

City, State, Zip

Web Site Address

2nd Mortgage Bank/Lending Instituiton

Company

Account #

Interest Rate | Payment Amount

Payment Address

City, State, Zip

Web Site Address

Equity Line

Company

Account #

Interest Rate | Payment Amount

Payment Address

City, State, Zip

Web Site Address

Company

Account #

Interest Rate | Payment Amount

Payment Address

City, State, Zip

Web Site Address

Company

Account #

Interest Rate | Payment Amount

Payment Address

City, State, Zip

Web Site Address

Company

Account #

Interest Rate | Payment Amount

Payment Address

City, State, Zip

Web Site Address

Websites

SITE	ID	LOGIN	PASSWORD HINT	EXPIRES
VRBO	652763 ASB	mysmokymtn	cat1	Cyber Mo
HomeAway	562363 CBTL		Cat1	Cyber Mon
webchalet			cat1	Cyber Mon
Edencrest			cat1	
Flip Key			Cat1	"
Trip Advisor			Cat1	"
mySmokymtnCabins				
Go Daddy				3yrs Cyber Mon 2017
VRBO	652763VB ASB			
Home Away	562363 VB			
VacationRentals.com				
	652763VB ASB			
	562363 CBTL			

Note: It is never a good idea to write down your passwords.

Websites

SITE	ID	LOGIN	PASSWORD HINT	EXPIRES

Note: It is never a good idea to write down your passwords.

Owner Network

me

HOME	VACATION HOME
Name Cindy Hannah	
Address	Address
City, State, Zip	City, State, Zip
Telephone 704-641-5761	Telephone
Cell Phone	Website
Email cindyhannah06@Gmail.com	Calendar Link

HOME	VACATION HOME
Name	
Address	Address
City, State, Zip	City, State, Zip
Telephone	Telephone
Cell Phone	Website
Email	Calendar Link

HOME	VACATION HOME
Name	
Address	Address
City, State, Zip	City, State, Zip
Telephone	Telephone
Cell Phone	Website
Email	Calendar Link

HOME	VACATION HOME
Name	
Address	Address
City, State, Zip	City, State, Zip
Telephone	Telephone
Cell Phone	Website
Email	Calendar Link

HOME	VACATION HOME
Name	
Address	Address
City, State, Zip	City, State, Zip
Telephone	Telephone
Cell Phone	Website
Email	Calendar Link

Owner Network

HOME	VACATION HOME
Name	
Address	Address
City, State, Zip	City, State, Zip
Telephone	Telephone
Cell Phone	Website
Email	Calendar Link

HOME	VACATION HOME
Name	
Address	Address
City, State, Zip	City, State, Zip
Telephone	Telephone
Cell Phone	Website
Email	Calendar Link

HOME	VACATION HOME
Name	
Address	Address
City, State, Zip	City, State, Zip
Telephone	Telephone
Cell Phone	Website
Email	Calendar Link

HOME	VACATION HOME
Name	
Address	Address
City, State, Zip	City, State, Zip
Telephone	Telephone
Cell Phone	Website
Email	Calendar Link

HOME	VACATION HOME
Name	
Address	Address
City, State, Zip	City, State, Zip
Telephone	Telephone
Cell Phone	Website
Email	Calendar Link

Owner Network

HOME		VACATION HOME	
Name	Trey Carmen & Nancy		Tammy & Jeff Pavarre
Address		Address	
City, State, Zip		City, State, Zip	
Telephone		Telephone	910-870-8193
Cell Phone	901-461-7933	Website	TuscanyhomesTN@yahoo
Email		Calendar Link	

HOME		VACATION HOME	
Name			
Address		Address	
City, State, Zip		City, State, Zip	
Telephone		Telephone	
Cell Phone		Website	
Email		Calendar Link	

HOME		VACATION HOME	
Name			
Address		Address	
City, State, Zip		City, State, Zip	
Telephone		Telephone	
Cell Phone		Website	
Email		Calendar Link	

HOME		VACATION HOME	
Name			
Address		Address	
City, State, Zip		City, State, Zip	
Telephone		Telephone	
Cell Phone		Website	
Email		Calendar Link	

HOME		VACATION HOME	
Name			
Address		Address	
City, State, Zip		City, State, Zip	
Telephone		Telephone	
Cell Phone		Website	
Email		Calendar Link	

Owner Network

HOME	VACATION HOME
Name	
Address	Address
City, State, Zip	City, State, Zip
Telephone	Telephone
Cell Phone	Website
Email	Calendar Link

HOME	VACATION HOME
Name	
Address	Address
City, State, Zip	City, State, Zip
Telephone	Telephone
Cell Phone	Website
Email	Calendar Link

HOME	VACATION HOME
Name	
Address	Address
City, State, Zip	City, State, Zip
Telephone	Telephone
Cell Phone	Website
Email	Calendar Link

HOME	VACATION HOME
Name	
Address	Address
City, State, Zip	City, State, Zip
Telephone	Telephone
Cell Phone	Website
Email	Calendar Link

HOME	VACATION HOME
Name	
Address	Address
City, State, Zip	City, State, Zip
Telephone	Telephone
Cell Phone	Website
Email	Calendar Link

Maid & Cleaning Companies

COMPANY

Name Tina Williams

Address

City, State, Zip

Telephone 865-

Cell Phone/Pager

Email

COMPANY

Name

Address

City, State, Zip

Telephone

Cell Phone/Pager

Email

COMPANY

Name

Address

City, State, Zip

Telephone

Cell Phone/Pager

Email

COMPANY

Name

Address

City, State, Zip

Telephone

Cell Phone/Pager

Email

COMPANY

Name

Address

City, State, Zip

Telephone

Cell Phone/Pager

Email

COMPANY

Name

Address

City, State, Zip

Telephone

Cell Phone/Pager

Email

COMPANY

Name

Address

City, State, Zip

Telephone

Cell Phone/Pager

Email

COMPANY

Name

Address

City, State, Zip

Telephone

Cell Phone/Pager

Email

COMPANY

Name

Address

City, State, Zip

Telephone

Cell Phone/Pager

Email

COMPANY

Name

Address

City, State, Zip

Telephone

Cell Phone/Pager

Email

Maid & Cleaning Companies

COMPANY

Name

Address

City, State, Zip

Telephone

Cell Phone/Pager

Email

COMPANY

Name

Address

City, State, Zip

Telephone

Cell Phone/Pager

Email

COMPANY

Name

Address

City, State, Zip

Telephone

Cell Phone/Pager

Email

COMPANY

Name

Address

City, State, Zip

Telephone

Cell Phone/Pager

Email

COMPANY

Name

Address

City, State, Zip

Telephone

Cell Phone/Pager

Email

COMPANY

Name

Address

City, State, Zip

Telephone

Cell Phone/Pager

Email

COMPANY

Name

Address

City, State, Zip

Telephone

Cell Phone/Pager

Email

COMPANY

Name

Address

City, State, Zip

Telephone

Cell Phone/Pager

Email

COMPANY

Name

Address

City, State, Zip

Telephone

Cell Phone/Pager

Email

COMPANY

Name

Address

City, State, Zip

Telephone

Cell Phone/Pager

Email

Utility Companies

POWER COMPANY

Name City of P. F. Water & Sewer
Address PO Box 1066
City, State, Zip Pigeon Forge TN 37868
Telephone 865-429-7375
Account # 0011-000 363-01

GAS COMPANY

Name
Address
City, State, Zip
Telephone
Account #

PROPANE

Name Holston Gas
Address
City, State, Zip
Telephone 865-575-1917
Account #

~~OIL~~ Propane

Name Suburban
Address
City, State, Zip
Telephone
Account #

WATER

Name
Address
City, State, Zip
Telephone
Account #

SEWER/SEPTIC

Name
Address
City, State, Zip
Telephone
Account #

CABLE/SATELLITE

Name Charter Communications
Address
City, State, Zip
Telephone 888-
Account #

TELEPHONE COMPANY

Name
Address
City, State, Zip
Telephone
Account #

TRASH/RUBBISH COMPANY

Name
Address
City, State, Zip
Telephone
Account #

OTHER

Name
Address
City, State, Zip
Telephone
Account #

Maintenance Companies

ELECTRICIAN

Company

Contact Person

Address

City, State, Zip

Telephone

Email

APPLIANCES

Company

Contact Person

Address

City, State, Zip

Telephone

Email

CARPET CLEANING

Company

Contact Person

Address

City, State, Zip

Telephone

Email

CARPENTER

Company ~~Eco Const.~~

Contact Person Fony Ogle

Address

City, State, Zip

Telephone

Email

LANDSCAPING

Company

Contact Person

Address

City, State, Zip

Telephone

Email

PLUMBER

Company

Contact Person

Address

City, State, Zip

Telephone

Email

HEATER/AIR

Company Johnny Veco

Contact Person

Address

City, State, Zip

Telephone

Email

ROOFING COMPANY

Company

Contact Person

Address

City, State, Zip

Telephone

Email

PAINTER

Company

Contact Person

Address

City, State, Zip

Telephone

Email

HANDYMAN

Company

Contact Person

Address

City, State, Zip

Telephone

Email

Maintenance Companies

COMPANY

Company CCO Const.

Contact Person Tony Ogle

Address

City, State, Zip

Telephone

Email

COMPANY

Company Heat & Air

Contact Person John Coleman

Address

City, State, Zip

Telephone 865-774-0671

Email

COMPANY

Company Multi-Code

Contact Person Kevin

Address

City, State, Zip

Telephone 865-454-2275

Email

COMPANY

Company Dardins Repair

Contact Person Hot Tub

Address

City, State, Zip

Telephone

Email

COMPANY

Company Tom Oakley

Contact Person maint.

Address

City, State, Zip

Telephone 865-850-0674

Email

COMPANY

Company Jim Otto

Contact Person TV

Address

City, State, Zip

Telephone 865-805-6859

Email

COMPANY

Company

Contact Person

Address

City, State, Zip

Telephone

Email

COMPANY

Company

Contact Person

Address

City, State, Zip

Telephone

Email

COMPANY

Company

Contact Person

Address

City, State, Zip

Telephone

Email

COMPANY

Company

Contact Person

Address

City, State, Zip

Telephone

Email

COMPANY

Company Jeff Harris

Contact Person

Address

City, State, Zip

Telephone 865-850-4820

Email

COMPANY

Company Plumber

Contact Person Marcus

Address

City, State, Zip

Telephone 865-712-2203

Email

COMPANY

Company

Contact Person

Address

City, State, Zip

Telephone

Email

COMPANY

Company

Contact Person

Address

City, State, Zip

Telephone

Email

COMPANY

Company

Contact Person

Address

City, State, Zip

Telephone

Email

COMPANY

Company Joey - Maintenance

Contact Person

Address

City, State, Zip

Telephone 865-255-8520

Email

COMPANY

Company

Contact Person

Address

City, State, Zip

Telephone

Email

COMPANY

Company

Contact Person

Address

City, State, Zip

Telephone

Email

COMPANY

Company

Contact Person

Address

City, State, Zip

Telephone

Email

COMPANY

Company Brothers Staining

Contact Person Dustin

Address

City, State, Zip

Telephone 865-322-2831

Email

Appliance Inventory

ITEM	MAKE	MODEL	MANUFACTURER	SERIAL #	LAST SERVICED
Washer					
Dryer					
Dishwasher					
Refrigerator					
Stove					
Microwave					
Heat					
Air Conditioner					
Computer	N/A				
Fax	None				
Printer	None				
Television					
VCR					
DVD					
Stereo					
CD Player					

ITEM	DESCRIPTION	QUANTITY	COST	ROOM	YEAR PURCHASED
Dishes	Corning	12	$150.00	Kitchen	1997
Ceiling Fan	Hunter	2	169.98	Bedrooms	2-20-14
"	Hunter-Rustic	1	180.00	Den	2-13-14
Floor lamp	Rustic	1	45.–	"	2-13-14
Shower Curt	Ivory Waffle	1	20.–	Master bath	2-13-14
wall sconce	Rustic Bronze	1	50.–	front porch	"
Shower Curt	Red Plaid	1	40.–	Guest Bath	"
Towels	Towels - baths	49 Total	235.42	Baths	2-15-14
Candle sticks	Red-Tower The	3	63.13	Den	2-1-14
Vase	Rustic vase w/balls	1	39.14	dining	

Property Inventory

ITEM	DESCRIPTION	QUANTITY	COST	ROOM	YEAR PURCHASED
Dishes	Corning	12	$150.00	Kitchen	1997

Property Inventory

ITEM	DESCRIPTION	QUANTITY	COST	ROOM	YEAR PURCHASED
Dishes	Corning	12	$150.00	Kitchen	1997

Date Dec 2014

DATE Dec 3, 2014	DATE	DATE 12-4-12-6	DATE Jan
Renter Information 12-23-28			
Name Mike Dye			
Address 6430 Adams ~~Circle~~ Center Dr			
426816 City, State, Zip Fort Worth TX			
Telephone 260-740-7613			
E-Mail summitcityroofing@comcast.net			
# of Nights 5			
____ Adults ____ Children			
# of Vehicles			
Tag #			
Pets No			
Referral Site			
Date Reserved 12-3			
Rate 280 Nite			
Fees 85 + 300			
Taxes 176.50			
Check List			
Sent Billing Agreement ☑	☐	☐	☐
Rental Rules ☑	☐	☐	☐
Directions ☐	☐	☐	☐
Deposit Returned ☐	☐	☐	☐
Rec. Deposit & Signed Rules ☐	☐	☐	☐
1st Payment ☐	☐	☐	☐
2nd Payment ☐	☐	☐	☐
4681 Scheduled Cleaning ☐	☐	☐	☐
Cleaning Feedback ☐	☐	☐	☐
WEEKLY TOTALS	**NIGHTLY TOTALS**	**NIGHTLY TOTALS**	**NIGHTLY TOTALS**
RENT 1400	**RENT**	**RENT**	**RENT**
TAXES 176.50	**TAXES**	**TAXES**	**TAXES**
CLEANING FEES 85	**CLEANING FEES**	**CLEANING FEES**	**CLEANING FEES**

Date ____________

DATE ____________	DATE ____________	DATE ____________	DATE ____________
❐	❐	❐	❐
❐	❐	❐	❐
❐	❐	❐	❐
❐	❐	❐	❐
❐	❐	❐	❐
❐	❐	❐	❐
❐	❐	❐	❐
❐	❐	❐	❐
❐	❐	❐	❐
NIGHTLY TOTALS	NIGHTLY TOTALS	NIGHTLY TOTALS	NIGHTLY TOTALS
RENT	RENT	RENT	RENT
TAXES	TAXES	TAXES	TAXES
CLEANING FEES	CLEANING FEES	CLEANING FEES	CLEANING FEES

Date ____________________

DATE____________________	DATE____________________	DATE____________________	DATE____________________
Renter Information			
Name			
Address			
City, State, Zip			
Telephone			
E-Mail			
# of Nights			
______ Adults ______ Children			
# of Vehicles			
Tag #			
Pets			
Referral Site			
Date Reserved			
Rate			
Fees			
Taxes			
Check List			
Sent Billing Agreement ❐	❐	❐	❐
Rental Rules ❐	❐	❐	❐
Directions ❐	❐	❐	❐
Deposit Returned ❐	❐	❐	❐
Rec. Deposit & Signed Rules ❐	❐	❐	❐
1st Payment ❐	❐	❐	❐
2nd Payment ❐	❐	❐	❐
Scheduled Cleaning ❐	❐	❐	❐
Cleaning Feedback ❐	❐	❐	❐
WEEKLY TOTALS	**NIGHTLY TOTALS**	**NIGHTLY TOTALS**	**NIGHTLY TOTALS**
RENT	**RENT**	**RENT**	**RENT**
TAXES	**TAXES**	**TAXES**	**TAXES**
CLEANING FEES	**CLEANING FEES**	**CLEANING FEES**	**CLEANING FEES**

Date ____________________

DATE ____________	DATE ____________	DATE ____________	DATE ____________
☐	☐	☐	☐
☐	☐	☐	☐
☐	☐	☐	☐
☐	☐	☐	☐
☐	☐	☐	☐
☐	☐	☐	☐
☐	☐	☐	☐
☐	☐	☐	☐
☐	☐	☐	☐
NIGHTLY TOTALS	NIGHTLY TOTALS	NIGHTLY TOTALS	NIGHTLY TOTALS
RENT	RENT	RENT	RENT
TAXES	TAXES	TAXES	TAXES
CLEANING FEES	CLEANING FEES	CLEANING FEES	CLEANING FEES

Date ____________

DATE ____________	DATE ____________	DATE ____________	DATE ____________
Renter Information			
Name			
Address			
City, State, Zip			
Telephone			
E-Mail			
# of Nights			
______ Adults ______ Children			
# of Vehicles			
Tag #			
Pets			
Referral Site			
Date Reserved			
Rate			
Fees			
Taxes			
Check List			
Sent Billing Agreement ☐	☐	☐	☐
Rental Rules ☐	☐	☐	☐
Directions ☐	☐	☐	☐
Deposit Returned ☐	☐	☐	☐
Rec. Deposit & Signed Rules ☐	☐	☐	☐
1st Payment ☐	☐	☐	☐
2nd Payment ☐	☐	☐	☐
Scheduled Cleaning ☐	☐	☐	☐
Cleaning Feedback ☐	☐	☐	☐
WEEKLY TOTALS	**NIGHTLY TOTALS**	**NIGHTLY TOTALS**	**NIGHTLY TOTALS**
RENT	**RENT**	**RENT**	**RENT**
TAXES	**TAXES**	**TAXES**	**TAXES**
CLEANING FEES	**CLEANING FEES**	**CLEANING FEES**	**CLEANING FEES**

Date ____________________

DATE __________	DATE __________	DATE __________	DATE __________
❐	❐	❐	❐
❐	❐	❐	❐
❐	❐	❐	❐
❐	❐	❐	❐
❐	❐	❐	❐
❐	❐	❐	❐
❐	❐	❐	❐
❐	❐	❐	❐
❐	❐	❐	❐
NIGHTLY TOTALS	NIGHTLY TOTALS	NIGHTLY TOTALS	NIGHTLY TOTALS
RENT	RENT	RENT	RENT
TAXES	TAXES	TAXES	TAXES
CLEANING FEES	CLEANING FEES	CLEANING FEES	CLEANING FEES

Date ____________________

DATE ____________	DATE ____________	DATE ____________	DATE ____________
Renter Information			
Name			
Address			
City, State, Zip			
Telephone			
E-Mail			
# of Nights			
______ Adults ______ Children			
# of Vehicles			
Tag #			
Pets			
Referral Site			
Date Reserved			
Rate			
Fees			
Taxes			
Check List			
Sent Billing Agreement ❐	❐	❐	❐
Rental Rules ❐	❐	❐	❐
Directions ❐	❐	❐	❐
Deposit Returned ❐	❐	❐	❐
Rec. Deposit & Signed Rules ❐	❐	❐	❐
1st Payment ❐	❐	❐	❐
2nd Payment ❐	❐	❐	❐
Scheduled Cleaning ❐	❐	❐	❐
Cleaning Feedback ❐	❐	❐	❐
WEEKLY TOTALS	**NIGHTLY TOTALS**	**NIGHTLY TOTALS**	**NIGHTLY TOTALS**
RENT	**RENT**	**RENT**	**RENT**
TAXES	**TAXES**	**TAXES**	**TAXES**
CLEANING FEES	**CLEANING FEES**	**CLEANING FEES**	**CLEANING FEES**

Date ______________________

DATE ____________	DATE ____________	DATE ____________	DATE ____________
☐	☐	☐	☐
☐	☐	☐	☐
☐	☐	☐	☐
☐	☐	☐	☐
☐	☐	☐	☐
☐	☐	☐	☐
☐	☐	☐	☐
☐	☐	☐	☐
☐	☐	☐	☐
NIGHTLY TOTALS	NIGHTLY TOTALS	NIGHTLY TOTALS	NIGHTLY TOTALS
RENT	RENT	RENT	RENT
TAXES	TAXES	TAXES	TAXES
CLEANING FEES	CLEANING FEES	CLEANING FEES	CLEANING FEES

Date ____________

DATE ____________	DATE ____________	DATE ____________	DATE ____________
Renter Information			
Name			
Address			
City, State, Zip			
Telephone			
E-Mail			
# of Nights			
______ Adults ______ Children			
# of Vehicles			
Tag #			
Pets			
Referral Site			
Date Reserved			
Rate			
Fees			
Taxes			
Check List			
Sent Billing Agreement ❐	❐	❐	❐
Rental Rules ❐	❐	❐	❐
Directions ❐	❐	❐	❐
Deposit Returned ❐	❐	❐	❐
Rec. Deposit & Signed Rules ❐	❐	❐	❐
1st Payment ❐	❐	❐	❐
2nd Payment ❐	❐	❐	❐
Scheduled Cleaning ❐	❐	❐	❐
Cleaning Feedback ❐	❐	❐	❐
WEEKLY TOTALS	**NIGHTLY TOTALS**	**NIGHTLY TOTALS**	**NIGHTLY TOTALS**
RENT	**RENT**	**RENT**	**RENT**
TAXES	**TAXES**	**TAXES**	**TAXES**
CLEANING FEES	**CLEANING FEES**	**CLEANING FEES**	**CLEANING FEES**

Date ______________

DATE ______________	DATE ______________	DATE ______________	DATE ______________
❐	❐	❐	❐
❐	❐	❐	❐
❐	❐	❐	❐
❐	❐	❐	❐
❐	❐	❐	❐
❐	❐	❐	❐
❐	❐	❐	❐
❐	❐	❐	❐
❐	❐	❐	❐
NIGHTLY TOTALS	NIGHTLY TOTALS	NIGHTLY TOTALS	NIGHTLY TOTALS
RENT	RENT	RENT	RENT
TAXES	TAXES	TAXES	TAXES
CLEANING FEES	CLEANING FEES	CLEANING FEES	CLEANING FEES

Date ______________

DATE ______________	DATE ______________	DATE ______________	DATE ______________
Renter Information			
Name			
Address			
City, State, Zip			
Telephone			
E-Mail			
# of Nights			
_____ Adults _____ Children			
# of Vehicles			
Tag #			
Pets			
Referral Site			
Date Reserved			
Rate			
Fees			
Taxes			
Check List			
Sent Billing Agreement ❒	❒	❒	❒
Rental Rules ❒	❒	❒	❒
Directions ❒	❒	❒	❒
Deposit Returned ❒	❒	❒	❒
Rec. Deposit & Signed Rules ❒	❒	❒	❒
1st Payment ❒	❒	❒	❒
2nd Payment ❒	❒	❒	❒
Scheduled Cleaning ❒	❒	❒	❒
Cleaning Feedback ❒	❒	❒	❒
WEEKLY TOTALS	**NIGHTLY TOTALS**	**NIGHTLY TOTALS**	**NIGHTLY TOTALS**
RENT	**RENT**	**RENT**	**RENT**
TAXES	**TAXES**	**TAXES**	**TAXES**
CLEANING FEES	**CLEANING FEES**	**CLEANING FEES**	**CLEANING FEES**

Date ____________

DATE ____________	DATE ____________	DATE ____________	DATE ____________
❒	❒	❒	❒
❒	❒	❒	❒
❒	❒	❒	❒
❒	❒	❒	❒
❒	❒	❒	❒
❒	❒	❒	❒
❒	❒	❒	❒
❒	❒	❒	❒
❒	❒	❒	❒
NIGHTLY TOTALS	NIGHTLY TOTALS	NIGHTLY TOTALS	NIGHTLY TOTALS
RENT	RENT	RENT	RENT
TAXES	TAXES	TAXES	TAXES
CLEANING FEES	CLEANING FEES	CLEANING FEES	CLEANING FEES

Date ____________________

DATE ____________	DATE ____________	DATE ____________	DATE ____________
Renter Information			
Name			
Address			
City, State, Zip			
Telephone			
E-Mail			
# of Nights			
______ Adults ______ Children			
# of Vehicles			
Tag #			
Pets			
Referral Site			
Date Reserved			
Rate			
Fees			
Taxes			
Check List			
Sent Billing Agreement ❐	❐	❐	❐
Rental Rules ❐	❐	❐	❐
Directions ❐	❐	❐	❐
Deposit Returned ❐	❐	❐	❐
Rec. Deposit & Signed Rules ❐	❐	❐	❐
1st Payment ❐	❐	❐	❐
2nd Payment ❐	❐	❐	❐
Scheduled Cleaning ❐	❐	❐	❐
Cleaning Feedback ❐	❐	❐	❐
WEEKLY TOTALS	**NIGHTLY TOTALS**	**NIGHTLY TOTALS**	**NIGHTLY TOTALS**
RENT	**RENT**	**RENT**	**RENT**
TAXES	**TAXES**	**TAXES**	**TAXES**
CLEANING FEES	**CLEANING FEES**	**CLEANING FEES**	**CLEANING FEES**

Date____________________

DATE____________	DATE____________	DATE____________	DATE____________
❒	❒	❒	❒
❒	❒	❒	❒
❒	❒	❒	❒
❒	❒	❒	❒
❒	❒	❒	❒
❒	❒	❒	❒
❒	❒	❒	❒
❒	❒	❒	❒
❒	❒	❒	❒
NIGHTLY TOTALS	NIGHTLY TOTALS	NIGHTLY TOTALS	NIGHTLY TOTALS
RENT	RENT	RENT	RENT
TAXES	TAXES	TAXES	TAXES
CLEANING FEES	CLEANING FEES	CLEANING FEES	CLEANING FEES

Date ____________

DATE ____________	DATE ____________	DATE ____________	DATE ____________
Renter Information			
Name			
Address			
City, State, Zip			
Telephone			
E-Mail			
# of Nights			
______ Adults ______ Children			
# of Vehicles			
Tag #			
Pets			
Referral Site			
Date Reserved			
Rate			
Fees			
Taxes			
Check List			
Sent Billing Agreement ❐	❐	❐	❐
Rental Rules ❐	❐	❐	❐
Directions ❐	❐	❐	❐
Deposit Returned ❐	❐	❐	❐
Rec. Deposit & Signed Rules ❐	❐	❐	❐
1st Payment ❐	❐	❐	❐
2nd Payment ❐	❐	❐	❐
Scheduled Cleaning ❐	❐	❐	❐
Cleaning Feedback ❐	❐	❐	❐
WEEKLY TOTALS	**NIGHTLY TOTALS**	**NIGHTLY TOTALS**	**NIGHTLY TOTALS**
RENT	**RENT**	**RENT**	**RENT**
TAXES	**TAXES**	**TAXES**	**TAXES**
CLEANING FEES	**CLEANING FEES**	**CLEANING FEES**	**CLEANING FEES**

Date__________________

DATE__________	DATE__________	DATE__________	DATE__________
❐	❐	❐	❐
❐	❐	❐	❐
❐	❐	❐	❐
❐	❐	❐	❐
❐	❐	❐	❐
❐	❐	❐	❐
❐	❐	❐	❐
❐	❐	❐	❐
❐	❐	❐	❐
NIGHTLY TOTALS	NIGHTLY TOTALS	NIGHTLY TOTALS	NIGHTLY TOTALS
RENT	RENT	RENT	RENT
TAXES	TAXES	TAXES	TAXES
CLEANING FEES	CLEANING FEES	CLEANING FEES	CLEANING FEES

Date ____________________

DATE ____________	DATE ____________	DATE ____________	DATE ____________
Renter Information			
Name			
Address			
City, State, Zip			
Telephone			
E-Mail			
# of Nights			
______ Adults ______ Children			
# of Vehicles			
Tag #			
Pets			
Referral Site			
Date Reserved			
Rate			
Fees			
Taxes			
Check List			
Sent Billing Agreement ❐	❐	❐	❐
Rental Rules ❐	❐	❐	❐
Directions ❐	❐	❐	❐
Deposit Returned ❐	❐	❐	❐
Rec. Deposit & Signed Rules ❐	❐	❐	❐
1st Payment ❐	❐	❐	❐
2nd Payment ❐	❐	❐	❐
Scheduled Cleaning ❐	❐	❐	❐
Cleaning Feedback ❐	❐	❐	❐
WEEKLY TOTALS	**NIGHTLY TOTALS**	**NIGHTLY TOTALS**	**NIGHTLY TOTALS**
RENT	**RENT**	**RENT**	**RENT**
TAXES	**TAXES**	**TAXES**	**TAXES**
CLEANING FEES	**CLEANING FEES**	**CLEANING FEES**	**CLEANING FEES**

Date ________________

DATE ________	DATE ________	DATE ________	DATE ________
❒	❒	❒	❒
❒	❒	❒	❒
❒	❒	❒	❒
❒	❒	❒	❒
❒	❒	❒	❒
❒	❒	❒	❒
❒	❒	❒	❒
❒	❒	❒	❒
❒	❒	❒	❒
NIGHTLY TOTALS	NIGHTLY TOTALS	NIGHTLY TOTALS	NIGHTLY TOTALS
RENT	RENT	RENT	RENT
TAXES	TAXES	TAXES	TAXES
CLEANING FEES	CLEANING FEES	CLEANING FEES	CLEANING FEES

Date ____________________

DATE ____________	DATE ____________	DATE ____________	DATE ____________
Renter Information			
Name			
Address			
City, State, Zip			
Telephone			
E-Mail			
# of Nights			
______ Adults ______ Children			
# of Vehicles			
Tag #			
Pets			
Referral Site			
Date Reserved			
Rate			
Fees			
Taxes			
Check List			
Sent Billing Agreement ☐	☐	☐	☐
Rental Rules ☐	☐	☐	☐
Directions ☐	☐	☐	☐
Deposit Returned ☐	☐	☐	☐
Rec. Deposit & Signed Rules ☐	☐	☐	☐
1st Payment ☐	☐	☐	☐
2nd Payment ☐	☐	☐	☐
Scheduled Cleaning ☐	☐	☐	☐
Cleaning Feedback ☐	☐	☐	☐
WEEKLY TOTALS	**NIGHTLY TOTALS**	**NIGHTLY TOTALS**	**NIGHTLY TOTALS**
RENT	**RENT**	**RENT**	**RENT**
TAXES	**TAXES**	**TAXES**	**TAXES**
CLEANING FEES	**CLEANING FEES**	**CLEANING FEES**	**CLEANING FEES**

Date ______________

DATE ______	DATE ______	DATE ______	DATE ______
❒	❒	❒	❒
❒	❒	❒	❒
❒	❒	❒	❒
❒	❒	❒	❒
❒	❒	❒	❒
❒	❒	❒	❒
❒	❒	❒	❒
❒	❒	❒	❒
❒	❒	❒	❒
NIGHTLY TOTALS	NIGHTLY TOTALS	NIGHTLY TOTALS	NIGHTLY TOTALS
RENT	RENT	RENT	RENT
TAXES	TAXES	TAXES	TAXES
CLEANING FEES	CLEANING FEES	CLEANING FEES	CLEANING FEES

*Date*______________

DATE________	DATE________	DATE________	DATE________
Renter Information			
Name			
Address			
City, State, Zip			
Telephone			
E-Mail			
# of Nights			
______ Adults ______ Children			
# of Vehicles			
Tag #			
Pets			
Referral Site			
Date Reserved			
Rate			
Fees			
Taxes			
Check List			
Sent Billing Agreement ❐	❐	❐	❐
Rental Rules ❐	❐	❐	❐
Directions ❐	❐	❐	❐
Deposit Returned ❐	❐	❐	❐
Rec. Deposit & Signed Rules ❐	❐	❐	❐
1st Payment ❐	❐	❐	❐
2nd Payment ❐	❐	❐	❐
Scheduled Cleaning ❐	❐	❐	❐
Cleaning Feedback ❐	❐	❐	❐
WEEKLY TOTALS	**NIGHTLY TOTALS**	**NIGHTLY TOTALS**	**NIGHTLY TOTALS**
RENT	**RENT**	**RENT**	**RENT**
TAXES	**TAXES**	**TAXES**	**TAXES**
CLEANING FEES	**CLEANING FEES**	**CLEANING FEES**	**CLEANING FEES**

*Date*________________

DATE__________	DATE__________	DATE__________	DATE__________
❐	❐	❐	❐
❐	❐	❐	❐
❐	❐	❐	❐
❐	❐	❐	❐
❐	❐	❐	❐
❐	❐	❐	❐
❐	❐	❐	❐
❐	❐	❐	❐
❐	❐	❐	❐
NIGHTLY TOTALS	NIGHTLY TOTALS	NIGHTLY TOTALS	NIGHTLY TOTALS
RENT	RENT	RENT	RENT
TAXES	TAXES	TAXES	TAXES
CLEANING FEES	CLEANING FEES	CLEANING FEES	CLEANING FEES

Date ____________________

DATE ____________	DATE ____________	DATE ____________	DATE ____________
Renter Information			
Name			
Address			
City, State, Zip			
Telephone			
E-Mail			
# of Nights			
______ Adults ______ Children			
# of Vehicles			
Tag #			
Pets			
Referral Site			
Date Reserved			
Rate			
Fees			
Taxes			
Check List			
Sent Billing Agreement ❐	❐	❐	❐
Rental Rules ❐	❐	❐	❐
Directions ❐	❐	❐	❐
Deposit Returned ❐	❐	❐	❐
Rec. Deposit & Signed Rules ❐	❐	❐	❐
1st Payment ❐	❐	❐	❐
2nd Payment ❐	❐	❐	❐
Scheduled Cleaning ❐	❐	❐	❐
Cleaning Feedback ❐	❐	❐	❐
WEEKLY TOTALS	**NIGHTLY TOTALS**	**NIGHTLY TOTALS**	**NIGHTLY TOTALS**
RENT	**RENT**	**RENT**	**RENT**
TAXES	**TAXES**	**TAXES**	**TAXES**
CLEANING FEES	**CLEANING FEES**	**CLEANING FEES**	**CLEANING FEES**

Date ____________________

DATE ____________	DATE ____________	DATE ____________	DATE ____________
❐	❐	❐	❐
❐	❐	❐	❐
❐	❐	❐	❐
❐	❐	❐	❐
❐	❐	❐	❐
❐	❐	❐	❐
❐	❐	❐	❐
❐	❐	❐	❐
❐	❐	❐	❐
NIGHTLY TOTALS	NIGHTLY TOTALS	NIGHTLY TOTALS	NIGHTLY TOTALS
RENT	RENT	RENT	RENT
TAXES	TAXES	TAXES	TAXES
CLEANING FEES	CLEANING FEES	CLEANING FEES	CLEANING FEES

Date ____________________

DATE________________	DATE________________	DATE________________	DATE________________
Renter Information			
Name			
Address			
City, State, Zip			
Telephone			
E-Mail			
# of Nights			
_____ Adults _____ Children			
# of Vehicles			
Tag #			
Pets			
Referral Site			
Date Reserved			
Rate			
Fees			
Taxes			
Check List			
Sent Billing Agreement ❐	❐	❐	❐
Rental Rules ❐	❐	❐	❐
Directions ❐	❐	❐	❐
Deposit Returned ❐	❐	❐	❐
Rec. Deposit & Signed Rules ❐	❐	❐	❐
1st Payment ❐	❐	❐	❐
2nd Payment ❐	❐	❐	❐
Scheduled Cleaning ❐	❐	❐	❐
Cleaning Feedback ❐	❐	❐	❐
WEEKLY TOTALS	**NIGHTLY TOTALS**	**NIGHTLY TOTALS**	**NIGHTLY TOTALS**
RENT	**RENT**	**RENT**	**RENT**
TAXES	**TAXES**	**TAXES**	**TAXES**
CLEANING FEES	**CLEANING FEES**	**CLEANING FEES**	**CLEANING FEES**

Date ______________

DATE ______	DATE ______	DATE ______	DATE ______
❐	❐	❐	❐
❐	❐	❐	❐
❐	❐	❐	❐
❐	❐	❐	❐
❐	❐	❐	❐
❐	❐	❐	❐
❐	❐	❐	❐
❐	❐	❐	❐
❐	❐	❐	❐
NIGHTLY TOTALS	NIGHTLY TOTALS	NIGHTLY TOTALS	NIGHTLY TOTALS
RENT	RENT	RENT	RENT
TAXES	TAXES	TAXES	TAXES
CLEANING FEES	CLEANING FEES	CLEANING FEES	CLEANING FEES

Date ______________

DATE ______________	DATE ______________	DATE ______________	DATE ______________
Renter Information			
Name			
Address			
City, State, Zip			
Telephone			
E-Mail			
# of Nights			
_____ Adults _____ Children			
# of Vehicles			
Tag #			
Pets			
Referral Site			
Date Reserved			
Rate			
Fees			
Taxes			
Check List			
Sent Billing Agreement ❐	❐	❐	❐
Rental Rules ❐	❐	❐	❐
Directions ❐	❐	❐	❐
Deposit Returned ❐	❐	❐	❐
Rec. Deposit & Signed Rules ❐	❐	❐	❐
1st Payment ❐	❐	❐	❐
2nd Payment ❐	❐	❐	❐
Scheduled Cleaning ❐	❐	❐	❐
Cleaning Feedback ❐	❐	❐	❐
WEEKLY TOTALS	**NIGHTLY TOTALS**	**NIGHTLY TOTALS**	**NIGHTLY TOTALS**
RENT	**RENT**	**RENT**	**RENT**
TAXES	**TAXES**	**TAXES**	**TAXES**
CLEANING FEES	**CLEANING FEES**	**CLEANING FEES**	**CLEANING FEES**

Date ______________

DATE ______	DATE ______	DATE ______	DATE ______
❐	❐	❐	❐
❐	❐	❐	❐
❐	❐	❐	❐
❐	❐	❐	❐
❐	❐	❐	❐
❐	❐	❐	❐
❐	❐	❐	❐
❐	❐	❐	❐
❐	❐	❐	❐
NIGHTLY TOTALS	NIGHTLY TOTALS	NIGHTLY TOTALS	NIGHTLY TOTALS
RENT	RENT	RENT	RENT
TAXES	TAXES	TAXES	TAXES
CLEANING FEES	CLEANING FEES	CLEANING FEES	CLEANING FEES

Date ____________________

DATE ____________	DATE ____________	DATE ____________	DATE ____________
Renter Information			
Name			
Address			
City, State, Zip			
Telephone			
E-Mail			
# of Nights			
______ Adults ______ Children			
# of Vehicles			
Tag #			
Pets			
Referral Site			
Date Reserved			
Rate			
Fees			
Taxes			
Check List			
Sent Billing Agreement ❐	❐	❐	❐
Rental Rules ❐	❐	❐	❐
Directions ❐	❐	❐	❐
Deposit Returned ❐	❐	❐	❐
Rec. Deposit & Signed Rules ❐	❐	❐	❐
1st Payment ❐	❐	❐	❐
2nd Payment ❐	❐	❐	❐
Scheduled Cleaning ❐	❐	❐	❐
Cleaning Feedback ❐	❐	❐	❐
WEEKLY TOTALS	**NIGHTLY TOTALS**	**NIGHTLY TOTALS**	**NIGHTLY TOTALS**
RENT	**RENT**	**RENT**	**RENT**
TAXES	**TAXES**	**TAXES**	**TAXES**
CLEANING FEES	**CLEANING FEES**	**CLEANING FEES**	**CLEANING FEES**

Date ______________

DATE ______	DATE ______	DATE ______	DATE ______
❐	❐	❐	❐
❐	❐	❐	❐
❐	❐	❐	❐
❐	❐	❐	❐
❐	❐	❐	❐
❐	❐	❐	❐
❐	❐	❐	❐
❐	❐	❐	❐
❐	❐	❐	❐
NIGHTLY TOTALS	NIGHTLY TOTALS	NIGHTLY TOTALS	NIGHTLY TOTALS
RENT	RENT	RENT	RENT
TAXES	TAXES	TAXES	TAXES
CLEANING FEES	CLEANING FEES	CLEANING FEES	CLEANING FEES

Date ____________

DATE ____________	DATE ____________	DATE ____________	DATE ____________
Renter Information			
Name			
Address			
City, State, Zip			
Telephone			
E-Mail			
# of Nights			
______ Adults ______ Children			
# of Vehicles			
Tag #			
Pets			
Referral Site			
Date Reserved			
Rate			
Fees			
Taxes			
Check List			
Sent Billing Agreement ❒	❒	❒	❒
Rental Rules ❒	❒	❒	❒
Directions ❒	❒	❒	❒
Deposit Returned ❒	❒	❒	❒
Rec. Deposit & Signed Rules ❒	❒	❒	❒
1st Payment ❒	❒	❒	❒
2nd Payment ❒	❒	❒	❒
Scheduled Cleaning ❒	❒	❒	❒
Cleaning Feedback ❒	❒	❒	❒
WEEKLY TOTALS	**NIGHTLY TOTALS**	**NIGHTLY TOTALS**	**NIGHTLY TOTALS**
RENT	**RENT**	**RENT**	**RENT**
TAXES	**TAXES**	**TAXES**	**TAXES**
CLEANING FEES	**CLEANING FEES**	**CLEANING FEES**	**CLEANING FEES**

Date ____________________

DATE ____________	DATE ____________	DATE ____________	DATE ____________
❐	❐	❐	❐
❐	❐	❐	❐
❐	❐	❐	❐
❐	❐	❐	❐
❐	❐	❐	❐
❐	❐	❐	❐
❐	❐	❐	❐
❐	❐	❐	❐
❐	❐	❐	❐
NIGHTLY TOTALS	NIGHTLY TOTALS	NIGHTLY TOTALS	NIGHTLY TOTALS
RENT	RENT	RENT	RENT
TAXES	TAXES	TAXES	TAXES
CLEANING FEES	CLEANING FEES	CLEANING FEES	CLEANING FEES

Date ____________

DATE ____________	DATE ____________	DATE ____________	DATE ____________
Renter Information			
Name			
Address			
City, State, Zip			
Telephone			
E-Mail			
# of Nights			
______ Adults ______ Children			
# of Vehicles			
Tag #			
Pets			
Referral Site			
Date Reserved			
Rate			
Fees			
Taxes			
Check List			
Sent Billing Agreement ☐	☐	☐	☐
Rental Rules ☐	☐	☐	☐
Directions ☐	☐	☐	☐
Deposit Returned ☐	☐	☐	☐
Rec. Deposit & Signed Rules ☐	☐	☐	☐
1st Payment ☐	☐	☐	☐
2nd Payment ☐	☐	☐	☐
Scheduled Cleaning ☐	☐	☐	☐
Cleaning Feedback ☐	☐	☐	☐
WEEKLY TOTALS	**NIGHTLY TOTALS**	**NIGHTLY TOTALS**	**NIGHTLY TOTALS**
RENT	**RENT**	**RENT**	**RENT**
TAXES	**TAXES**	**TAXES**	**TAXES**
CLEANING FEES	**CLEANING FEES**	**CLEANING FEES**	**CLEANING FEES**

Date ____________________

DATE ____________	DATE ____________	DATE ____________	DATE ____________
☐	☐	☐	☐
☐	☐	☐	☐
☐	☐	☐	☐
☐	☐	☐	☐
☐	☐	☐	☐
☐	☐	☐	☐
☐	☐	☐	☐
☐	☐	☐	☐
☐	☐	☐	☐
NIGHTLY TOTALS	NIGHTLY TOTALS	NIGHTLY TOTALS	NIGHTLY TOTALS
RENT	RENT	RENT	RENT
TAXES	TAXES	TAXES	TAXES
CLEANING FEES	CLEANING FEES	CLEANING FEES	CLEANING FEES

Date ____________________

DATE ____________________	DATE ____________________	DATE ____________________	DATE ____________________
Renter Information			
Name			
Address			
City, State, Zip			
Telephone			
E-Mail			
# of Nights			
______ Adults ______ Children			
# of Vehicles			
Tag #			
Pets			
Referral Site			
Date Reserved			
Rate			
Fees			
Taxes			
Check List			
Sent Billing Agreement ❐	❐	❐	❐
Rental Rules ❐	❐	❐	❐
Directions ❐	❐	❐	❐
Deposit Returned ❐	❐	❐	❐
Rec. Deposit & Signed Rules ❐	❐	❐	❐
1st Payment ❐	❐	❐	❐
2nd Payment ❐	❐	❐	❐
Scheduled Cleaning ❐	❐	❐	❐
Cleaning Feedback ❐	❐	❐	❐
WEEKLY TOTALS	**NIGHTLY TOTALS**	**NIGHTLY TOTALS**	**NIGHTLY TOTALS**
RENT	**RENT**	**RENT**	**RENT**
TAXES	**TAXES**	**TAXES**	**TAXES**
CLEANING FEES	**CLEANING FEES**	**CLEANING FEES**	**CLEANING FEES**

Date ____________

DATE ________	DATE ________	DATE ________	DATE ________
❐	❐	❐	❐
❐	❐	❐	❐
❐	❐	❐	❐
❐	❐	❐	❐
❐	❐	❐	❐
❐	❐	❐	❐
❐	❐	❐	❐
❐	❐	❐	❐
❐	❐	❐	❐
NIGHTLY TOTALS	NIGHTLY TOTALS	NIGHTLY TOTALS	NIGHTLY TOTALS
RENT	RENT	RENT	RENT
TAXES	TAXES	TAXES	TAXES
CLEANING FEES	CLEANING FEES	CLEANING FEES	CLEANING FEES

Date ____________________

DATE ____________	DATE ____________	DATE ____________	DATE ____________
Renter Information			
Name			
Address			
City, State, Zip			
Telephone			
E-Mail			
# of Nights			
______ Adults ______ Children			
# of Vehicles			
Tag #			
Pets			
Referral Site			
Date Reserved			
Rate			
Fees			
Taxes			
Check List			
Sent Billing Agreement ❐	❐	❐	❐
Rental Rules ❐	❐	❐	❐
Directions ❐	❐	❐	❐
Deposit Returned ❐	❐	❐	❐
Rec. Deposit & Signed Rules ❐	❐	❐	❐
1st Payment ❐	❐	❐	❐
2nd Payment ❐	❐	❐	❐
Scheduled Cleaning ❐	❐	❐	❐
Cleaning Feedback ❐	❐	❐	❐

WEEKLY TOTALS	NIGHTLY TOTALS	NIGHTLY TOTALS	NIGHTLY TOTALS
RENT	RENT	RENT	RENT
TAXES	TAXES	TAXES	TAXES
CLEANING FEES	CLEANING FEES	CLEANING FEES	CLEANING FEES

Date________________

DATE________________	DATE________________	DATE________________	DATE________________
❐	❐	❐	❐
❐	❐	❐	❐
❐	❐	❐	❐
❐	❐	❐	❐
❐	❐	❐	❐
❐	❐	❐	❐
❐	❐	❐	❐
❐	❐	❐	❐
❐	❐	❐	❐
NIGHTLY TOTALS	NIGHTLY TOTALS	NIGHTLY TOTALS	NIGHTLY TOTALS
RENT	RENT	RENT	RENT
TAXES	TAXES	TAXES	TAXES
CLEANING FEES	CLEANING FEES	CLEANING FEES	CLEANING FEES

Date ____________________

DATE ____________________	DATE ____________________	DATE ____________________	DATE ____________________
Renter Information			
Name			
Address			
City, State, Zip			
Telephone			
E-Mail			
# of Nights			
_____ Adults _____ Children			
# of Vehicles			
Tag #			
Pets			
Referral Site			
Date Reserved			
Rate			
Fees			
Taxes			
Check List			
Sent Billing Agreement ❐	❐	❐	❐
Rental Rules ❐	❐	❐	❐
Directions ❐	❐	❐	❐
Deposit Returned ❐	❐	❐	❐
Rec. Deposit & Signed Rules ❐	❐	❐	❐
1st Payment ❐	❐	❐	❐
2nd Payment ❐	❐	❐	❐
Scheduled Cleaning ❐	❐	❐	❐
Cleaning Feedback ❐	❐	❐	❐
WEEKLY TOTALS	**NIGHTLY TOTALS**	**NIGHTLY TOTALS**	**NIGHTLY TOTALS**
RENT	**RENT**	**RENT**	**RENT**
TAXES	**TAXES**	**TAXES**	**TAXES**
CLEANING FEES	**CLEANING FEES**	**CLEANING FEES**	**CLEANING FEES**

Date ______________

DATE ______	DATE ______	DATE ______	DATE ______
❐	❐	❐	❐
❐	❐	❐	❐
❐	❐	❐	❐
❐	❐	❐	❐
❐	❐	❐	❐
❐	❐	❐	❐
❐	❐	❐	❐
❐	❐	❐	❐
❐	❐	❐	❐
NIGHTLY TOTALS	NIGHTLY TOTALS	NIGHTLY TOTALS	NIGHTLY TOTALS
RENT	RENT	RENT	RENT
TAXES	TAXES	TAXES	TAXES
CLEANING FEES	CLEANING FEES	CLEANING FEES	CLEANING FEES

Date ____________________

DATE____________________	DATE____________________	DATE____________________	DATE____________________
Renter Information			
Name			
Address			
City, State, Zip			
Telephone			
E-Mail			
# of Nights			
______ Adults ______ Children			
# of Vehicles			
Tag #			
Pets			
Referral Site			
Date Reserved			
Rate			
Fees			
Taxes			
Check List			
Sent Billing Agreement ❐	❐	❐	❐
Rental Rules ❐	❐	❐	❐
Directions ❐	❐	❐	❐
Deposit Returned ❐	❐	❐	❐
Rec. Deposit & Signed Rules ❐	❐	❐	❐
1st Payment ❐	❐	❐	❐
2nd Payment ❐	❐	❐	❐
Scheduled Cleaning ❐	❐	❐	❐
Cleaning Feedback ❐	❐	❐	❐
WEEKLY TOTALS	**NIGHTLY TOTALS**	**NIGHTLY TOTALS**	**NIGHTLY TOTALS**
RENT	**RENT**	**RENT**	**RENT**
TAXES	**TAXES**	**TAXES**	**TAXES**
CLEANING FEES	**CLEANING FEES**	**CLEANING FEES**	**CLEANING FEES**

Date ____________

DATE ______	DATE ______	DATE ______	DATE ______
❐	❐	❐	❐
❐	❐	❐	❐
❐	❐	❐	❐
❐	❐	❐	❐
❐	❐	❐	❐
❐	❐	❐	❐
❐	❐	❐	❐
❐	❐	❐	❐
❐	❐	❐	❐
NIGHTLY TOTALS	NIGHTLY TOTALS	NIGHTLY TOTALS	NIGHTLY TOTALS
RENT	RENT	RENT	RENT
TAXES	TAXES	TAXES	TAXES
CLEANING FEES	CLEANING FEES	CLEANING FEES	CLEANING FEES

Date___________________

DATE___________________	DATE___________________	DATE___________________	DATE___________________
Renter Information			
Name			
Address			
City, State, Zip			
Telephone			
E-Mail			
# of Nights			
______ Adults ______ Children			
# of Vehicles			
Tag #			
Pets			
Referral Site			
Date Reserved			
Rate			
Fees			
Taxes			
Check List			
Sent Billing Agreement ❒	❒	❒	❒
Rental Rules ❒	❒	❒	❒
Directions ❒	❒	❒	❒
Deposit Returned ❒	❒	❒	❒
Rec. Deposit & Signed Rules ❒	❒	❒	❒
1st Payment ❒	❒	❒	❒
2nd Payment ❒	❒	❒	❒
Scheduled Cleaning ❒	❒	❒	❒
Cleaning Feedback ❒	❒	❒	❒
WEEKLY TOTALS	**NIGHTLY TOTALS**	**NIGHTLY TOTALS**	**NIGHTLY TOTALS**
RENT	**RENT**	**RENT**	**RENT**
TAXES	**TAXES**	**TAXES**	**TAXES**
CLEANING FEES	**CLEANING FEES**	**CLEANING FEES**	**CLEANING FEES**

Date ______________

DATE ______	DATE ______	DATE ______	DATE ______
❒	❒	❒	❒
❒	❒	❒	❒
❒	❒	❒	❒
❒	❒	❒	❒
❒	❒	❒	❒
❒	❒	❒	❒
❒	❒	❒	❒
❒	❒	❒	❒
❒	❒	❒	❒
NIGHTLY TOTALS	NIGHTLY TOTALS	NIGHTLY TOTALS	NIGHTLY TOTALS
RENT	RENT	RENT	RENT
TAXES	TAXES	TAXES	TAXES
CLEANING FEES	CLEANING FEES	CLEANING FEES	CLEANING FEES

Date ____________

DATE ____________	DATE ____________	DATE ____________	DATE ____________
Renter Information			
Name			
Address			
City, State, Zip			
Telephone			
E-Mail			
# of Nights			
______ Adults ______ Children			
# of Vehicles			
Tag #			
Pets			
Referral Site			
Date Reserved			
Rate			
Fees			
Taxes			
Check List			
Sent Billing Agreement ❐	❐	❐	❐
Rental Rules ❐	❐	❐	❐
Directions ❐	❐	❐	❐
Deposit Returned ❐	❐	❐	❐
Rec. Deposit & Signed Rules ❐	❐	❐	❐
1st Payment ❐	❐	❐	❐
2nd Payment ❐	❐	❐	❐
Scheduled Cleaning ❐	❐	❐	❐
Cleaning Feedback ❐	❐	❐	❐

WEEKLY TOTALS	NIGHTLY TOTALS	NIGHTLY TOTALS	NIGHTLY TOTALS
RENT	RENT	RENT	RENT
TAXES	TAXES	TAXES	TAXES
CLEANING FEES	CLEANING FEES	CLEANING FEES	CLEANING FEES

Date ______________

DATE ______	DATE ______	DATE ______	DATE ______
☐	☐	☐	☐
☐	☐	☐	☐
☐	☐	☐	☐
☐	☐	☐	☐
☐	☐	☐	☐
☐	☐	☐	☐
☐	☐	☐	☐
☐	☐	☐	☐
☐	☐	☐	☐
NIGHTLY TOTALS	NIGHTLY TOTALS	NIGHTLY TOTALS	NIGHTLY TOTALS
RENT	RENT	RENT	RENT
TAXES	TAXES	TAXES	TAXES
CLEANING FEES	CLEANING FEES	CLEANING FEES	CLEANING FEES

Date ____________________

DATE ____________	DATE ____________	DATE ____________	DATE ____________
Renter Information			
Name			
Address			
City, State, Zip			
Telephone			
E-Mail			
# of Nights			
______ Adults ______ Children			
# of Vehicles			
Tag #			
Pets			
Referral Site			
Date Reserved			
Rate			
Fees			
Taxes			
Check List			
Sent Billing Agreement ❐	❐	❐	❐
Rental Rules ❐	❐	❐	❐
Directions ❐	❐	❐	❐
Deposit Returned ❐	❐	❐	❐
Rec. Deposit & Signed Rules ❐	❐	❐	❐
1st Payment ❐	❐	❐	❐
2nd Payment ❐	❐	❐	❐
Scheduled Cleaning ❐	❐	❐	❐
Cleaning Feedback ❐	❐	❐	❐
WEEKLY TOTALS	**NIGHTLY TOTALS**	**NIGHTLY TOTALS**	**NIGHTLY TOTALS**
RENT	**RENT**	**RENT**	**RENT**
TAXES	**TAXES**	**TAXES**	**TAXES**
CLEANING FEES	**CLEANING FEES**	**CLEANING FEES**	**CLEANING FEES**

Date ____________________

DATE ____________	DATE ____________	DATE ____________	DATE ____________
❑	❑	❑	❑
❑	❑	❑	❑
❑	❑	❑	❑
❑	❑	❑	❑
❑	❑	❑	❑
❑	❑	❑	❑
❑	❑	❑	❑
❑	❑	❑	❑
❑	❑	❑	❑
NIGHTLY TOTALS	NIGHTLY TOTALS	NIGHTLY TOTALS	NIGHTLY TOTALS
RENT	RENT	RENT	RENT
TAXES	TAXES	TAXES	TAXES
CLEANING FEES	CLEANING FEES	CLEANING FEES	CLEANING FEES

Date ____________________

DATE ____________________	DATE ____________________	DATE ____________________	DATE ____________________
Renter Information			
Name			
Address			
City, State, Zip			
Telephone			
E-Mail			
# of Nights			
_____ Adults _____ Children			
# of Vehicles			
Tag #			
Pets			
Referral Site			
Date Reserved			
Rate			
Fees			
Taxes			
Check List			
Sent Billing Agreement ❐	❐	❐	❐
Rental Rules ❐	❐	❐	❐
Directions ❐	❐	❐	❐
Deposit Returned ❐	❐	❐	❐
Rec. Deposit & Signed Rules ❐	❐	❐	❐
1st Payment ❐	❐	❐	❐
2nd Payment ❐	❐	❐	❐
Scheduled Cleaning ❐	❐	❐	❐
Cleaning Feedback ❐	❐	❐	❐
WEEKLY TOTALS	**NIGHTLY TOTALS**	**NIGHTLY TOTALS**	**NIGHTLY TOTALS**
RENT	**RENT**	**RENT**	**RENT**
TAXES	**TAXES**	**TAXES**	**TAXES**
CLEANING FEES	**CLEANING FEES**	**CLEANING FEES**	**CLEANING FEES**

Date ______________

DATE______	DATE______	DATE______	DATE______
❐	❐	❐	❐
❐	❐	❐	❐
❐	❐	❐	❐
❐	❐	❐	❐
❐	❐	❐	❐
❐	❐	❐	❐
❐	❐	❐	❐
❐	❐	❐	❐
❐	❐	❐	❐
NIGHTLY TOTALS	NIGHTLY TOTALS	NIGHTLY TOTALS	NIGHTLY TOTALS
RENT	RENT	RENT	RENT
TAXES	TAXES	TAXES	TAXES
CLEANING FEES	CLEANING FEES	CLEANING FEES	CLEANING FEES

Date ______________________

DATE__________	DATE__________	DATE__________	DATE__________
Renter Information			
Name			
Address			
City, State, Zip			
Telephone			
E-Mail			
# of Nights			
______ Adults ______ Children			
# of Vehicles			
Tag #			
Pets			
Referral Site			
Date Reserved			
Rate			
Fees			
Taxes			
Check List			
Sent Billing Agreement ❐	❐	❐	❐
Rental Rules ❐	❐	❐	❐
Directions ❐	❐	❐	❐
Deposit Returned ❐	❐	❐	❐
Rec. Deposit & Signed Rules ❐	❐	❐	❐
1st Payment ❐	❐	❐	❐
2nd Payment ❐	❐	❐	❐
Scheduled Cleaning ❐	❐	❐	❐
Cleaning Feedback ❐	❐	❐	❐
WEEKLY TOTALS	**NIGHTLY TOTALS**	**NIGHTLY TOTALS**	**NIGHTLY TOTALS**
RENT	**RENT**	**RENT**	**RENT**
TAXES	**TAXES**	**TAXES**	**TAXES**
CLEANING FEES	**CLEANING FEES**	**CLEANING FEES**	**CLEANING FEES**

Date ______________

DATE ______	DATE ______	DATE ______	DATE ______
❐	❐	❐	❐
❐	❐	❐	❐
❐	❐	❐	❐
❐	❐	❐	❐
❐	❐	❐	❐
❐	❐	❐	❐
❐	❐	❐	❐
❐	❐	❐	❐
❐	❐	❐	❐
NIGHTLY TOTALS	NIGHTLY TOTALS	NIGHTLY TOTALS	NIGHTLY TOTALS
RENT	RENT	RENT	RENT
TAXES	TAXES	TAXES	TAXES
CLEANING FEES	CLEANING FEES	CLEANING FEES	CLEANING FEES

Date ____________

DATE ____________	DATE ____________	DATE ____________	DATE ____________
Renter Information			
Name			
Address			
City, State, Zip			
Telephone			
E-Mail			
# of Nights			
______ Adults ______ Children			
# of Vehicles			
Tag #			
Pets			
Referral Site			
Date Reserved			
Rate			
Fees			
Taxes			
Check List			
Sent Billing Agreement ☐	☐	☐	☐
Rental Rules ☐	☐	☐	☐
Directions ☐	☐	☐	☐
Deposit Returned ☐	☐	☐	☐
Rec. Deposit & Signed Rules ☐	☐	☐	☐
1st Payment ☐	☐	☐	☐
2nd Payment ☐	☐	☐	☐
Scheduled Cleaning ☐	☐	☐	☐
Cleaning Feedback ☐	☐	☐	☐
WEEKLY TOTALS	**NIGHTLY TOTALS**	**NIGHTLY TOTALS**	**NIGHTLY TOTALS**
RENT	**RENT**	**RENT**	**RENT**
TAXES	**TAXES**	**TAXES**	**TAXES**
CLEANING FEES	**CLEANING FEES**	**CLEANING FEES**	**CLEANING FEES**

Date ______________________

DATE ______________	DATE ______________	DATE ______________	DATE ______________
❐	❐	❐	❐
❐	❐	❐	❐
❐	❐	❐	❐
❐	❐	❐	❐
❐	❐	❐	❐
❐	❐	❐	❐
❐	❐	❐	❐
❐	❐	❐	❐
❐	❐	❐	❐
NIGHTLY TOTALS	NIGHTLY TOTALS	NIGHTLY TOTALS	NIGHTLY TOTALS
RENT	RENT	RENT	RENT
TAXES	TAXES	TAXES	TAXES
CLEANING FEES	CLEANING FEES	CLEANING FEES	CLEANING FEES

Date ____________________

DATE ____________	DATE ____________	DATE ____________	DATE ____________
Renter Information			
Name			
Address			
City, State, Zip			
Telephone			
E-Mail			
# of Nights			
______ Adults ______ Children			
# of Vehicles			
Tag #			
Pets			
Referral Site			
Date Reserved			
Rate			
Fees			
Taxes			
Check List			
Sent Billing Agreement ❐	❐	❐	❐
Rental Rules ❐	❐	❐	❐
Directions ❐	❐	❐	❐
Deposit Returned ❐	❐	❐	❐
Rec. Deposit & Signed Rules ❐	❐	❐	❐
1st Payment ❐	❐	❐	❐
2nd Payment ❐	❐	❐	❐
Scheduled Cleaning ❐	❐	❐	❐
Cleaning Feedback ❐	❐	❐	❐
WEEKLY TOTALS	**NIGHTLY TOTALS**	**NIGHTLY TOTALS**	**NIGHTLY TOTALS**
RENT	**RENT**	**RENT**	**RENT**
TAXES	**TAXES**	**TAXES**	**TAXES**
CLEANING FEES	**CLEANING FEES**	**CLEANING FEES**	**CLEANING FEES**

Date ________________

DATE ____________	DATE ____________	DATE ____________	DATE ____________
❐	❐	❐	❐
❐	❐	❐	❐
❐	❐	❐	❐
❐	❐	❐	❐
❐	❐	❐	❐
❐	❐	❐	❐
❐	❐	❐	❐
❐	❐	❐	❐
❐	❐	❐	❐
NIGHTLY TOTALS	NIGHTLY TOTALS	NIGHTLY TOTALS	NIGHTLY TOTALS
RENT	RENT	RENT	RENT
TAXES	TAXES	TAXES	TAXES
CLEANING FEES	CLEANING FEES	CLEANING FEES	CLEANING FEES

Date____________________

DATE__________	DATE__________	DATE__________	DATE__________
Renter Information			
Name			
Address			
City, State, Zip			
Telephone			
E-Mail			
# of Nights			
_____ Adults _____ Children			
# of Vehicles			
Tag #			
Pets			
Referral Site			
Date Reserved			
Rate			
Fees			
Taxes			
Check List			
Sent Billing Agreement ❐	❐	❐	❐
Rental Rules ❐	❐	❐	❐
Directions ❐	❐	❐	❐
Deposit Returned ❐	❐	❐	❐
Rec. Deposit & Signed Rules ❐	❐	❐	❐
1st Payment ❐	❐	❐	❐
2nd Payment ❐	❐	❐	❐
Scheduled Cleaning ❐	❐	❐	❐
Cleaning Feedback ❐	❐	❐	❐
WEEKLY TOTALS	**NIGHTLY TOTALS**	**NIGHTLY TOTALS**	**NIGHTLY TOTALS**
RENT	**RENT**	**RENT**	**RENT**
TAXES	**TAXES**	**TAXES**	**TAXES**
CLEANING FEES	**CLEANING FEES**	**CLEANING FEES**	**CLEANING FEES**

Date ____________

DATE ____________	DATE ____________	DATE ____________	DATE ____________
❐	❐	❐	❐
❐	❐	❐	❐
❐	❐	❐	❐
❐	❐	❐	❐
❐	❐	❐	❐
❐	❐	❐	❐
❐	❐	❐	❐
❐	❐	❐	❐
❐	❐	❐	❐
NIGHTLY TOTALS	NIGHTLY TOTALS	NIGHTLY TOTALS	NIGHTLY TOTALS
RENT	RENT	RENT	RENT
TAXES	TAXES	TAXES	TAXES
CLEANING FEES	CLEANING FEES	CLEANING FEES	CLEANING FEES

Date ____________________

DATE ____________	DATE ____________	DATE ____________	DATE ____________
Renter Information			
Name			
Address			
City, State, Zip			
Telephone			
E-Mail			
# of Nights			
_____ Adults _____ Children			
# of Vehicles			
Tag #			
Pets			
Referral Site			
Date Reserved			
Rate			
Fees			
Taxes			
Check List			
Sent Billing Agreement ❐	❐	❐	❐
Rental Rules ❐	❐	❐	❐
Directions ❐	❐	❐	❐
Deposit Returned ❐	❐	❐	❐
Rec. Deposit & Signed Rules ❐	❐	❐	❐
1st Payment ❐	❐	❐	❐
2nd Payment ❐	❐	❐	❐
Scheduled Cleaning ❐	❐	❐	❐
Cleaning Feedback ❐	❐	❐	❐
WEEKLY TOTALS	**NIGHTLY TOTALS**	**NIGHTLY TOTALS**	**NIGHTLY TOTALS**
RENT	**RENT**	**RENT**	**RENT**
TAXES	**TAXES**	**TAXES**	**TAXES**
CLEANING FEES	**CLEANING FEES**	**CLEANING FEES**	**CLEANING FEES**

Date ____________

DATE ________	DATE ________	DATE ________	DATE ________
❒	❒	❒	❒
❒	❒	❒	❒
❒	❒	❒	❒
❒	❒	❒	❒
❒	❒	❒	❒
❒	❒	❒	❒
❒	❒	❒	❒
❒	❒	❒	❒
❒	❒	❒	❒
NIGHTLY TOTALS	NIGHTLY TOTALS	NIGHTLY TOTALS	NIGHTLY TOTALS
RENT	RENT	RENT	RENT
TAXES	TAXES	TAXES	TAXES
CLEANING FEES	CLEANING FEES	CLEANING FEES	CLEANING FEES

Date_______________

DATE__________	DATE__________	DATE__________	DATE__________
Renter Information			
Name			
Address			
City, State, Zip			
Telephone			
E-Mail			
# of Nights			
_____ Adults _____ Children			
# of Vehicles			
Tag #			
Pets			
Referral Site			
Date Reserved			
Rate			
Fees			
Taxes			
Check List			
Sent Billing Agreement ❐	❐	❐	❐
Rental Rules ❐	❐	❐	❐
Directions ❐	❐	❐	❐
Deposit Returned ❐	❐	❐	❐
Rec. Deposit & Signed Rules ❐	❐	❐	❐
1st Payment ❐	❐	❐	❐
2nd Payment ❐	❐	❐	❐
Scheduled Cleaning ❐	❐	❐	❐
Cleaning Feedback ❐	❐	❐	❐
WEEKLY TOTALS	**NIGHTLY TOTALS**	**NIGHTLY TOTALS**	**NIGHTLY TOTALS**
RENT	**RENT**	**RENT**	**RENT**
TAXES	**TAXES**	**TAXES**	**TAXES**
CLEANING FEES	**CLEANING FEES**	**CLEANING FEES**	**CLEANING FEES**

Date ____________________

DATE ________	DATE ________	DATE ________	DATE ________
❐	❐	❐	❐
❐	❐	❐	❐
❐	❐	❐	❐
❐	❐	❐	❐
❐	❐	❐	❐
❐	❐	❐	❐
❐	❐	❐	❐
❐	❐	❐	❐
❐	❐	❐	❐
NIGHTLY TOTALS	NIGHTLY TOTALS	NIGHTLY TOTALS	NIGHTLY TOTALS
RENT	RENT	RENT	RENT
TAXES	TAXES	TAXES	TAXES
CLEANING FEES	CLEANING FEES	CLEANING FEES	CLEANING FEES

Date ____________

DATE ____________	DATE ____________	DATE ____________	DATE ____________
Renter Information			
Name			
Address			
City, State, Zip			
Telephone			
E-Mail			
# of Nights			
______ Adults ______ Children			
# of Vehicles			
Tag #			
Pets			
Referral Site			
Date Reserved			
Rate			
Fees			
Taxes			
Check List			
Sent Billing Agreement ❐	❐	❐	❐
Rental Rules ❐	❐	❐	❐
Directions ❐	❐	❐	❐
Deposit Returned ❐	❐	❐	❐
Rec. Deposit & Signed Rules ❐	❐	❐	❐
1st Payment ❐	❐	❐	❐
2nd Payment ❐	❐	❐	❐
Scheduled Cleaning ❐	❐	❐	❐
Cleaning Feedback ❐	❐	❐	❐
WEEKLY TOTALS	**NIGHTLY TOTALS**	**NIGHTLY TOTALS**	**NIGHTLY TOTALS**
RENT	**RENT**	**RENT**	**RENT**
TAXES	**TAXES**	**TAXES**	**TAXES**
CLEANING FEES	**CLEANING FEES**	**CLEANING FEES**	**CLEANING FEES**

Date ______________

DATE ______	DATE ______	DATE ______	DATE ______
❐	❐	❐	❐
❐	❐	❐	❐
❐	❐	❐	❐
❐	❐	❐	❐
❐	❐	❐	❐
❐	❐	❐	❐
❐	❐	❐	❐
❐	❐	❐	❐
❐	❐	❐	❐
NIGHTLY TOTALS	NIGHTLY TOTALS	NIGHTLY TOTALS	NIGHTLY TOTALS
RENT	RENT	RENT	RENT
TAXES	TAXES	TAXES	TAXES
CLEANING FEES	CLEANING FEES	CLEANING FEES	CLEANING FEES

Date ____________________

DATE____________	DATE____________	DATE____________	DATE____________
Renter Information			
Name			
Address			
City, State, Zip			
Telephone			
E-Mail			
# of Nights			
______ Adults ______ Children			
# of Vehicles			
Tag #			
Pets			
Referral Site			
Date Reserved			
Rate			
Fees			
Taxes			
Check List			
Sent Billing Agreement ❐	❐	❐	❐
Rental Rules ❐	❐	❐	❐
Directions ❐	❐	❐	❐
Deposit Returned ❐	❐	❐	❐
Rec. Deposit & Signed Rules ❐	❐	❐	❐
1st Payment ❐	❐	❐	❐
2nd Payment ❐	❐	❐	❐
Scheduled Cleaning ❐	❐	❐	❐
Cleaning Feedback ❐	❐	❐	❐
WEEKLY TOTALS	**NIGHTLY TOTALS**	**NIGHTLY TOTALS**	**NIGHTLY TOTALS**
RENT	**RENT**	**RENT**	**RENT**
TAXES	**TAXES**	**TAXES**	**TAXES**
CLEANING FEES	**CLEANING FEES**	**CLEANING FEES**	**CLEANING FEES**

Date________________

DATE________	DATE________	DATE________	DATE________
❐	❐	❐	❐
❐	❐	❐	❐
❐	❐	❐	❐
❐	❐	❐	❐
❐	❐	❐	❐
❐	❐	❐	❐
❐	❐	❐	❐
❐	❐	❐	❐
❐	❐	❐	❐
NIGHTLY TOTALS	NIGHTLY TOTALS	NIGHTLY TOTALS	NIGHTLY TOTALS
RENT	RENT	RENT	RENT
TAXES	TAXES	TAXES	TAXES
CLEANING FEES	CLEANING FEES	CLEANING FEES	CLEANING FEES

Date ________________

DATE ____________	DATE ____________	DATE ____________	DATE ____________
Renter Information			
Name			
Address			
City, State, Zip			
Telephone			
E-Mail			
# of Nights			
_____ Adults _____ Children			
# of Vehicles			
Tag #			
Pets			
Referral Site			
Date Reserved			
Rate			
Fees			
Taxes			
Check List			
Sent Billing Agreement ❐	❐	❐	❐
Rental Rules ❐	❐	❐	❐
Directions ❐	❐	❐	❐
Deposit Returned ❐	❐	❐	❐
Rec. Deposit & Signed Rules ❐	❐	❐	❐
1st Payment ❐	❐	❐	❐
2nd Payment ❐	❐	❐	❐
Scheduled Cleaning ❐	❐	❐	❐
Cleaning Feedback ❐	❐	❐	❐
WEEKLY TOTALS	**NIGHTLY TOTALS**	**NIGHTLY TOTALS**	**NIGHTLY TOTALS**
RENT	**RENT**	**RENT**	**RENT**
TAXES	**TAXES**	**TAXES**	**TAXES**
CLEANING FEES	**CLEANING FEES**	**CLEANING FEES**	**CLEANING FEES**

*Date*________________

DATE________	DATE________	DATE________	DATE________
❐	❐	❐	❐
❐	❐	❐	❐
❐	❐	❐	❐
❐	❐	❐	❐
❐	❐	❐	❐
❐	❐	❐	❐
❐	❐	❐	❐
❐	❐	❐	❐
❐	❐	❐	❐
NIGHTLY TOTALS	NIGHTLY TOTALS	NIGHTLY TOTALS	NIGHTLY TOTALS
RENT	RENT	RENT	RENT
TAXES	TAXES	TAXES	TAXES
CLEANING FEES	CLEANING FEES	CLEANING FEES	CLEANING FEES

Date ____________________

DATE ____________	DATE ____________	DATE ____________	DATE ____________
Renter Information			
Name			
Address			
City, State, Zip			
Telephone			
E-Mail			
# of Nights			
______ Adults ______ Children			
# of Vehicles			
Tag #			
Pets			
Referral Site			
Date Reserved			
Rate			
Fees			
Taxes			
Check List			
Sent Billing Agreement ❒	❒	❒	❒
Rental Rules ❒	❒	❒	❒
Directions ❒	❒	❒	❒
Deposit Returned ❒	❒	❒	❒
Rec. Deposit & Signed Rules ❒	❒	❒	❒
1st Payment ❒	❒	❒	❒
2nd Payment ❒	❒	❒	❒
Scheduled Cleaning ❒	❒	❒	❒
Cleaning Feedback ❒	❒	❒	❒
WEEKLY TOTALS	**NIGHTLY TOTALS**	**NIGHTLY TOTALS**	**NIGHTLY TOTALS**
RENT	**RENT**	**RENT**	**RENT**
TAXES	**TAXES**	**TAXES**	**TAXES**
CLEANING FEES	**CLEANING FEES**	**CLEANING FEES**	**CLEANING FEES**

Date ______________

DATE ______	DATE ______	DATE ______	DATE ______
❒	❒	❒	❒
❒	❒	❒	❒
❒	❒	❒	❒
❒	❒	❒	❒
❒	❒	❒	❒
❒	❒	❒	❒
❒	❒	❒	❒
❒	❒	❒	❒
❒	❒	❒	❒
NIGHTLY TOTALS	NIGHTLY TOTALS	NIGHTLY TOTALS	NIGHTLY TOTALS
RENT	RENT	RENT	RENT
TAXES	TAXES	TAXES	TAXES
CLEANING FEES	CLEANING FEES	CLEANING FEES	CLEANING FEES

Date ____________________

DATE__________	DATE__________	DATE__________	DATE__________
Renter Information			
Name			
Address			
City, State, Zip			
Telephone			
E-Mail			
# of Nights			
______ Adults ______ Children			
# of Vehicles			
Tag #			
Pets			
Referral Site			
Date Reserved			
Rate			
Fees			
Taxes			
Check List			
Sent Billing Agreement ❐	❐	❐	❐
Rental Rules ❐	❐	❐	❐
Directions ❐	❐	❐	❐
Deposit Returned ❐	❐	❐	❐
Rec. Deposit & Signed Rules ❐	❐	❐	❐
1st Payment ❐	❐	❐	❐
2nd Payment ❐	❐	❐	❐
Scheduled Cleaning ❐	❐	❐	❐
Cleaning Feedback ❐	❐	❐	❐
WEEKLY TOTALS	**NIGHTLY TOTALS**	**NIGHTLY TOTALS**	**NIGHTLY TOTALS**
RENT	**RENT**	**RENT**	**RENT**
TAXES	**TAXES**	**TAXES**	**TAXES**
CLEANING FEES	**CLEANING FEES**	**CLEANING FEES**	**CLEANING FEES**

Date ____________________

DATE ____________	DATE ____________	DATE ____________	DATE ____________
❐	❐	❐	❐
❐	❐	❐	❐
❐	❐	❐	❐
❐	❐	❐	❐
❐	❐	❐	❐
❐	❐	❐	❐
❐	❐	❐	❐
❐	❐	❐	❐
❐	❐	❐	❐
NIGHTLY TOTALS	NIGHTLY TOTALS	NIGHTLY TOTALS	NIGHTLY TOTALS
RENT	RENT	RENT	RENT
TAXES	TAXES	TAXES	TAXES
CLEANING FEES	CLEANING FEES	CLEANING FEES	CLEANING FEES

Date ____________

DATE ____________	DATE ____________	DATE ____________	DATE ____________
Renter Information			
Name			
Address			
City, State, Zip			
Telephone			
E-Mail			
# of Nights			
______ Adults ______ Children			
# of Vehicles			
Tag #			
Pets			
Referral Site			
Date Reserved			
Rate			
Fees			
Taxes			
Check List			
Sent Billing Agreement ❐	❐	❐	❐
Rental Rules ❐	❐	❐	❐
Directions ❐	❐	❐	❐
Deposit Returned ❐	❐	❐	❐
Rec. Deposit & Signed Rules ❐	❐	❐	❐
1st Payment ❐	❐	❐	❐
2nd Payment ❐	❐	❐	❐
Scheduled Cleaning ❐	❐	❐	❐
Cleaning Feedback ❐	❐	❐	❐
WEEKLY TOTALS	**NIGHTLY TOTALS**	**NIGHTLY TOTALS**	**NIGHTLY TOTALS**
RENT	**RENT**	**RENT**	**RENT**
TAXES	**TAXES**	**TAXES**	**TAXES**
CLEANING FEES	**CLEANING FEES**	**CLEANING FEES**	**CLEANING FEES**

Date ______________________

DATE ____________	DATE ____________	DATE ____________	DATE ____________
❐	❐	❐	❐
❐	❐	❐	❐
❐	❐	❐	❐
❐	❐	❐	❐
❐	❐	❐	❐
❐	❐	❐	❐
❐	❐	❐	❐
❐	❐	❐	❐
❐	❐	❐	❐
NIGHTLY TOTALS	NIGHTLY TOTALS	NIGHTLY TOTALS	NIGHTLY TOTALS
RENT	RENT	RENT	RENT
TAXES	TAXES	TAXES	TAXES
CLEANING FEES	CLEANING FEES	CLEANING FEES	CLEANING FEES

*Date*__________________

DATE__________________	DATE__________________	DATE__________________	DATE__________________
Renter Information			
Name			
Address			
City, State, Zip			
Telephone			
E-Mail			
# of Nights			
______ Adults ______ Children			
# of Vehicles			
Tag #			
Pets			
Referral Site			
Date Reserved			
Rate			
Fees			
Taxes			
Check List			
Sent Billing Agreement ❐	❐	❐	❐
Rental Rules ❐	❐	❐	❐
Directions ❐	❐	❐	❐
Deposit Returned ❐	❐	❐	❐
Rec. Deposit & Signed Rules ❐	❐	❐	❐
1st Payment ❐	❐	❐	❐
2nd Payment ❐	❐	❐	❐
Scheduled Cleaning ❐	❐	❐	❐
Cleaning Feedback ❐	❐	❐	❐
WEEKLY TOTALS	**NIGHTLY TOTALS**	**NIGHTLY TOTALS**	**NIGHTLY TOTALS**
RENT	**RENT**	**RENT**	**RENT**
TAXES	**TAXES**	**TAXES**	**TAXES**
CLEANING FEES	**CLEANING FEES**	**CLEANING FEES**	**CLEANING FEES**

Date ____________________

DATE ____________	DATE ____________	DATE ____________	DATE ____________
❐	❐	❐	❐
❐	❐	❐	❐
❐	❐	❐	❐
❐	❐	❐	❐
❐	❐	❐	❐
❐	❐	❐	❐
❐	❐	❐	❐
❐	❐	❐	❐
❐	❐	❐	❐
NIGHTLY TOTALS	NIGHTLY TOTALS	NIGHTLY TOTALS	NIGHTLY TOTALS
RENT	RENT	RENT	RENT
TAXES	TAXES	TAXES	TAXES
CLEANING FEES	CLEANING FEES	CLEANING FEES	CLEANING FEES

Date ____________

DATE ____________	DATE ____________	DATE ____________	DATE ____________
Renter Information			
Name			
Address			
City, State, Zip			
Telephone			
E-Mail			
# of Nights			
______ Adults ______ Children			
# of Vehicles			
Tag #			
Pets			
Referral Site			
Date Reserved			
Rate			
Fees			
Taxes			
Check List			
Sent Billing Agreement ❐	❐	❐	❐
Rental Rules ❐	❐	❐	❐
Directions ❐	❐	❐	❐
Deposit Returned ❐	❐	❐	❐
Rec. Deposit & Signed Rules ❐	❐	❐	❐
1st Payment ❐	❐	❐	❐
2nd Payment ❐	❐	❐	❐
Scheduled Cleaning ❐	❐	❐	❐
Cleaning Feedback ❐	❐	❐	❐
WEEKLY TOTALS	**NIGHTLY TOTALS**	**NIGHTLY TOTALS**	**NIGHTLY TOTALS**
RENT	**RENT**	**RENT**	**RENT**
TAXES	**TAXES**	**TAXES**	**TAXES**
CLEANING FEES	**CLEANING FEES**	**CLEANING FEES**	**CLEANING FEES**

Date______________

DATE__________	DATE__________	DATE__________	DATE__________
❐	❐	❐	❐
❐	❐	❐	❐
❐	❐	❐	❐
❐	❐	❐	❐
❐	❐	❐	❐
❐	❐	❐	❐
❐	❐	❐	❐
❐	❐	❐	❐
❐	❐	❐	❐
NIGHTLY TOTALS	NIGHTLY TOTALS	NIGHTLY TOTALS	NIGHTLY TOTALS
RENT	RENT	RENT	RENT
TAXES	TAXES	TAXES	TAXES
CLEANING FEES	CLEANING FEES	CLEANING FEES	CLEANING FEES

Date ____________________

DATE ____________	DATE ____________	DATE ____________	DATE ____________
Renter Information			
Name			
Address			
City, State, Zip			
Telephone			
E-Mail			
# of Nights			
______ Adults ______ Children			
# of Vehicles			
Tag #			
Pets			
Referral Site			
Date Reserved			
Rate			
Fees			
Taxes			
Check List			
Sent Billing Agreement ☐	☐	☐	☐
Rental Rules ☐	☐	☐	☐
Directions ☐	☐	☐	☐
Deposit Returned ☐	☐	☐	☐
Rec. Deposit & Signed Rules ☐	☐	☐	☐
1st Payment ☐	☐	☐	☐
2nd Payment ☐	☐	☐	☐
Scheduled Cleaning ☐	☐	☐	☐
Cleaning Feedback ☐	☐	☐	☐
WEEKLY TOTALS	**NIGHTLY TOTALS**	**NIGHTLY TOTALS**	**NIGHTLY TOTALS**
RENT	**RENT**	**RENT**	**RENT**
TAXES	**TAXES**	**TAXES**	**TAXES**
CLEANING FEES	**CLEANING FEES**	**CLEANING FEES**	**CLEANING FEES**

*Date*___________________

DATE__________	DATE__________	DATE__________	DATE__________
❐	❐	❐	❐
❐	❐	❐	❐
❐	❐	❐	❐
❐	❐	❐	❐
❐	❐	❐	❐
❐	❐	❐	❐
❐	❐	❐	❐
❐	❐	❐	❐
❐	❐	❐	❐
NIGHTLY TOTALS	NIGHTLY TOTALS	NIGHTLY TOTALS	NIGHTLY TOTALS
RENT	RENT	RENT	RENT
TAXES	TAXES	TAXES	TAXES
CLEANING FEES	CLEANING FEES	CLEANING FEES	CLEANING FEES

Date ______________

DATE ______________	DATE ______________	DATE ______________	DATE ______________
Renter Information			
Name			
Address			
City, State, Zip			
Telephone			
E-Mail			
# of Nights			
_____ Adults _____ Children			
# of Vehicles			
Tag #			
Pets			
Referral Site			
Date Reserved			
Rate			
Fees			
Taxes			
Check List			
Sent Billing Agreement ❐	❐	❐	❐
Rental Rules ❐	❐	❐	❐
Directions ❐	❐	❐	❐
Deposit Returned ❐	❐	❐	❐
Rec. Deposit & Signed Rules ❐	❐	❐	❐
1st Payment ❐	❐	❐	❐
2nd Payment ❐	❐	❐	❐
Scheduled Cleaning ❐	❐	❐	❐
Cleaning Feedback ❐	❐	❐	❐

WEEKLY TOTALS	NIGHTLY TOTALS	NIGHTLY TOTALS	NIGHTLY TOTALS
RENT	RENT	RENT	RENT
TAXES	TAXES	TAXES	TAXES
CLEANING FEES	CLEANING FEES	CLEANING FEES	CLEANING FEES

Date ______________

DATE ______	DATE ______	DATE ______	DATE ______
❐	❐	❐	❐
❐	❐	❐	❐
❐	❐	❐	❐
❐	❐	❐	❐
❐	❐	❐	❐
❐	❐	❐	❐
❐	❐	❐	❐
❐	❐	❐	❐
❐	❐	❐	❐
NIGHTLY TOTALS	NIGHTLY TOTALS	NIGHTLY TOTALS	NIGHTLY TOTALS
RENT	RENT	RENT	RENT
TAXES	TAXES	TAXES	TAXES
CLEANING FEES	CLEANING FEES	CLEANING FEES	CLEANING FEES

*Date*________________

DATE__________	DATE__________	DATE__________	DATE__________
Renter Information			
Name			
Address			
City, State, Zip			
Telephone			
E-Mail			
# of Nights			
_____ Adults _____ Children			
# of Vehicles			
Tag #			
Pets			
Referral Site			
Date Reserved			
Rate			
Fees			
Taxes			
Check List			
Sent Billing Agreement ❐	❐	❐	❐
Rental Rules ❐	❐	❐	❐
Directions ❐	❐	❐	❐
Deposit Returned ❐	❐	❐	❐
Rec. Deposit & Signed Rules ❐	❐	❐	❐
1st Payment ❐	❐	❐	❐
2nd Payment ❐	❐	❐	❐
Scheduled Cleaning ❐	❐	❐	❐
Cleaning Feedback ❐	❐	❐	❐
WEEKLY TOTALS	**NIGHTLY TOTALS**	**NIGHTLY TOTALS**	**NIGHTLY TOTALS**
RENT	**RENT**	**RENT**	**RENT**
TAXES	**TAXES**	**TAXES**	**TAXES**
CLEANING FEES	**CLEANING FEES**	**CLEANING FEES**	**CLEANING FEES**

Date ______________

DATE ______________	DATE ______________	DATE ______________	DATE ______________
❐	❐	❐	❐
❐	❐	❐	❐
❐	❐	❐	❐
❐	❐	❐	❐
❐	❐	❐	❐
❐	❐	❐	❐
❐	❐	❐	❐
❐	❐	❐	❐
❐	❐	❐	❐
NIGHTLY TOTALS	NIGHTLY TOTALS	NIGHTLY TOTALS	NIGHTLY TOTALS
RENT	RENT	RENT	RENT
TAXES	TAXES	TAXES	TAXES
CLEANING FEES	CLEANING FEES	CLEANING FEES	CLEANING FEES

Date ____________________

DATE ____________	DATE ____________	DATE ____________	DATE ____________
Renter Information			
Name			
Address			
City, State, Zip			
Telephone			
E-Mail			
# of Nights			
______ Adults ______ Children			
# of Vehicles			
Tag #			
Pets			
Referral Site			
Date Reserved			
Rate			
Fees			
Taxes			
Check List			
Sent Billing Agreement ❐	❐	❐	❐
Rental Rules ❐	❐	❐	❐
Directions ❐	❐	❐	❐
Deposit Returned ❐	❐	❐	❐
Rec. Deposit & Signed Rules ❐	❐	❐	❐
1st Payment ❐	❐	❐	❐
2nd Payment ❐	❐	❐	❐
Scheduled Cleaning ❐	❐	❐	❐
Cleaning Feedback ❐	❐	❐	❐
WEEKLY TOTALS	**NIGHTLY TOTALS**	**NIGHTLY TOTALS**	**NIGHTLY TOTALS**
RENT	**RENT**	**RENT**	**RENT**
TAXES	**TAXES**	**TAXES**	**TAXES**
CLEANING FEES	**CLEANING FEES**	**CLEANING FEES**	**CLEANING FEES**

Date ____________________

DATE ____________	DATE ____________	DATE ____________	DATE ____________
☐	☐	☐	☐
☐	☐	☐	☐
☐	☐	☐	☐
☐	☐	☐	☐
☐	☐	☐	☐
☐	☐	☐	☐
☐	☐	☐	☐
☐	☐	☐	☐
☐	☐	☐	☐
NIGHTLY TOTALS	NIGHTLY TOTALS	NIGHTLY TOTALS	NIGHTLY TOTALS
RENT	RENT	RENT	RENT
TAXES	TAXES	TAXES	TAXES
CLEANING FEES	CLEANING FEES	CLEANING FEES	CLEANING FEES

Date ____________________

DATE ____________________	DATE ____________________	DATE ____________________	DATE ____________________
Renter Information			
Name			
Address			
City, State, Zip			
Telephone			
E-Mail			
# of Nights			
______ Adults ______ Children			
# of Vehicles			
Tag #			
Pets			
Referral Site			
Date Reserved			
Rate			
Fees			
Taxes			
Check List			
Sent Billing Agreement ❐	❐	❐	❐
Rental Rules ❐	❐	❐	❐
Directions ❐	❐	❐	❐
Deposit Returned ❐	❐	❐	❐
Rec. Deposit & Signed Rules ❐	❐	❐	❐
1st Payment ❐	❐	❐	❐
2nd Payment ❐	❐	❐	❐
Scheduled Cleaning ❐	❐	❐	❐
Cleaning Feedback ❐	❐	❐	❐

WEEKLY TOTALS	NIGHTLY TOTALS	NIGHTLY TOTALS	NIGHTLY TOTALS
RENT	RENT	RENT	RENT
TAXES	TAXES	TAXES	TAXES
CLEANING FEES	CLEANING FEES	CLEANING FEES	CLEANING FEES

Date ____________

DATE ____________	DATE ____________	DATE ____________	DATE ____________
❐	❐	❐	❐
❐	❐	❐	❐
❐	❐	❐	❐
❐	❐	❐	❐
❐	❐	❐	❐
❐	❐	❐	❐
❐	❐	❐	❐
❐	❐	❐	❐
❐	❐	❐	❐
NIGHTLY TOTALS	NIGHTLY TOTALS	NIGHTLY TOTALS	NIGHTLY TOTALS
RENT	RENT	RENT	RENT
TAXES	TAXES	TAXES	TAXES
CLEANING FEES	CLEANING FEES	CLEANING FEES	CLEANING FEES

*Date*______________

DATE______	DATE______	DATE______	DATE______
Renter Information			
Name			
Address			
City, State, Zip			
Telephone			
E-Mail			
# of Nights			
______ Adults ______ Children			
# of Vehicles			
Tag #			
Pets			
Referral Site			
Date Reserved			
Rate			
Fees			
Taxes			
Check List			
Sent Billing Agreement ❐	❐	❐	❐
Rental Rules ❐	❐	❐	❐
Directions ❐	❐	❐	❐
Deposit Returned ❐	❐	❐	❐
Rec. Deposit & Signed Rules ❐	❐	❐	❐
1st Payment ❐	❐	❐	❐
2nd Payment ❐	❐	❐	❐
Scheduled Cleaning ❐	❐	❐	❐
Cleaning Feedback ❐	❐	❐	❐
WEEKLY TOTALS	**NIGHTLY TOTALS**	**NIGHTLY TOTALS**	**NIGHTLY TOTALS**
RENT	**RENT**	**RENT**	**RENT**
TAXES	**TAXES**	**TAXES**	**TAXES**
CLEANING FEES	**CLEANING FEES**	**CLEANING FEES**	**CLEANING FEES**

Date ____________________

DATE________	DATE________	DATE________	DATE________
❐	❐	❐	❐
❐	❐	❐	❐
❐	❐	❐	❐
❐	❐	❐	❐
❐	❐	❐	❐
❐	❐	❐	❐
❐	❐	❐	❐
❐	❐	❐	❐
❐	❐	❐	❐
NIGHTLY TOTALS	NIGHTLY TOTALS	NIGHTLY TOTALS	NIGHTLY TOTALS
RENT	RENT	RENT	RENT
TAXES	TAXES	TAXES	TAXES
CLEANING FEES	CLEANING FEES	CLEANING FEES	CLEANING FEES

Date ____________________

DATE ____________	DATE ____________	DATE ____________	DATE ____________
Renter Information			
Name			
Address			
City, State, Zip			
Telephone			
E-Mail			
# of Nights			
_____ Adults _____ Children			
# of Vehicles			
Tag #			
Pets			
Referral Site			
Date Reserved			
Rate			
Fees			
Taxes			
Check List			
Sent Billing Agreement ☐	☐	☐	☐
Rental Rules ☐	☐	☐	☐
Directions ☐	☐	☐	☐
Deposit Returned ☐	☐	☐	☐
Rec. Deposit & Signed Rules ☐	☐	☐	☐
1st Payment ☐	☐	☐	☐
2nd Payment ☐	☐	☐	☐
Scheduled Cleaning ☐	☐	☐	☐
Cleaning Feedback ☐	☐	☐	☐
WEEKLY TOTALS	**NIGHTLY TOTALS**	**NIGHTLY TOTALS**	**NIGHTLY TOTALS**
RENT	**RENT**	**RENT**	**RENT**
TAXES	**TAXES**	**TAXES**	**TAXES**
CLEANING FEES	**CLEANING FEES**	**CLEANING FEES**	**CLEANING FEES**

Date ____________

DATE ____________	DATE ____________	DATE ____________	DATE ____________
❐	❐	❐	❐
❐	❐	❐	❐
❐	❐	❐	❐
❐	❐	❐	❐
❐	❐	❐	❐
❐	❐	❐	❐
❐	❐	❐	❐
❐	❐	❐	❐
❐	❐	❐	❐
NIGHTLY TOTALS	NIGHTLY TOTALS	NIGHTLY TOTALS	NIGHTLY TOTALS
RENT	RENT	RENT	RENT
TAXES	TAXES	TAXES	TAXES
CLEANING FEES	CLEANING FEES	CLEANING FEES	CLEANING FEES

Date ____________

DATE ____________	DATE ____________	DATE ____________	DATE ____________
Renter Information			
Name			
Address			
City, State, Zip			
Telephone			
E-Mail			
# of Nights			
______ Adults ______ Children			
# of Vehicles			
Tag #			
Pets			
Referral Site			
Date Reserved			
Rate			
Fees			
Taxes			
Check List			
Sent Billing Agreement ❐	❐	❐	❐
Rental Rules ❐	❐	❐	❐
Directions ❐	❐	❐	❐
Deposit Returned ❐	❐	❐	❐
Rec. Deposit & Signed Rules ❐	❐	❐	❐
1st Payment ❐	❐	❐	❐
2nd Payment ❐	❐	❐	❐
Scheduled Cleaning ❐	❐	❐	❐
Cleaning Feedback ❐	❐	❐	❐
WEEKLY TOTALS	**NIGHTLY TOTALS**	**NIGHTLY TOTALS**	**NIGHTLY TOTALS**
RENT	**RENT**	**RENT**	**RENT**
TAXES	**TAXES**	**TAXES**	**TAXES**
CLEANING FEES	**CLEANING FEES**	**CLEANING FEES**	**CLEANING FEES**

Date ____________

DATE ____________	DATE ____________	DATE ____________	DATE ____________
❐	❐	❐	❐
❐	❐	❐	❐
❐	❐	❐	❐
❐	❐	❐	❐
❐	❐	❐	❐
❐	❐	❐	❐
❐	❐	❐	❐
❐	❐	❐	❐
❐	❐	❐	❐
NIGHTLY TOTALS	NIGHTLY TOTALS	NIGHTLY TOTALS	NIGHTLY TOTALS
RENT	RENT	RENT	RENT
TAXES	TAXES	TAXES	TAXES
CLEANING FEES	CLEANING FEES	CLEANING FEES	CLEANING FEES

Date ____________

DATE ____________	DATE ____________	DATE ____________	DATE ____________
Renter Information			
Name			
Address			
City, State, Zip			
Telephone			
E-Mail			
# of Nights			
_____ Adults _____ Children			
# of Vehicles			
Tag #			
Pets			
Referral Site			
Date Reserved			
Rate			
Fees			
Taxes			
Check List			
Sent Billing Agreement ❐	❐	❐	❐
Rental Rules ❐	❐	❐	❐
Directions ❐	❐	❐	❐
Deposit Returned ❐	❐	❐	❐
Rec. Deposit & Signed Rules ❐	❐	❐	❐
1st Payment ❐	❐	❐	❐
2nd Payment ❐	❐	❐	❐
Scheduled Cleaning ❐	❐	❐	❐
Cleaning Feedback ❐	❐	❐	❐
WEEKLY TOTALS	**NIGHTLY TOTALS**	**NIGHTLY TOTALS**	**NIGHTLY TOTALS**
RENT	**RENT**	**RENT**	**RENT**
TAXES	**TAXES**	**TAXES**	**TAXES**
CLEANING FEES	**CLEANING FEES**	**CLEANING FEES**	**CLEANING FEES**

Date ____________

DATE ________	DATE ________	DATE ________	DATE ________
❐	❐	❐	❐
❐	❐	❐	❐
❐	❐	❐	❐
❐	❐	❐	❐
❐	❐	❐	❐
❐	❐	❐	❐
❐	❐	❐	❐
❐	❐	❐	❐
❐	❐	❐	❐
NIGHTLY TOTALS	NIGHTLY TOTALS	NIGHTLY TOTALS	NIGHTLY TOTALS
RENT	RENT	RENT	RENT
TAXES	TAXES	TAXES	TAXES
CLEANING FEES	CLEANING FEES	CLEANING FEES	CLEANING FEES

Date ____________

DATE ____________	DATE ____________	DATE ____________	DATE ____________
Renter Information			
Name			
Address			
City, State, Zip			
Telephone			
E-Mail			
# of Nights			
______ Adults ______ Children			
# of Vehicles			
Tag #			
Pets			
Referral Site			
Date Reserved			
Rate			
Fees			
Taxes			
Check List			
Sent Billing Agreement ❐	❐	❐	❐
Rental Rules ❐	❐	❐	❐
Directions ❐	❐	❐	❐
Deposit Returned ❐	❐	❐	❐
Rec. Deposit & Signed Rules ❐	❐	❐	❐
1st Payment ❐	❐	❐	❐
2nd Payment ❐	❐	❐	❐
Scheduled Cleaning ❐	❐	❐	❐
Cleaning Feedback ❐	❐	❐	❐

WEEKLY TOTALS	NIGHTLY TOTALS	NIGHTLY TOTALS	NIGHTLY TOTALS
RENT	RENT	RENT	RENT
TAXES	TAXES	TAXES	TAXES
CLEANING FEES	CLEANING FEES	CLEANING FEES	CLEANING FEES

Date ______________________

DATE ________	DATE ________	DATE ________	DATE ________
❐	❐	❐	❐
❐	❐	❐	❐
❐	❐	❐	❐
❐	❐	❐	❐
❐	❐	❐	❐
❐	❐	❐	❐
❐	❐	❐	❐
❐	❐	❐	❐
❐	❐	❐	❐
NIGHTLY TOTALS	NIGHTLY TOTALS	NIGHTLY TOTALS	NIGHTLY TOTALS
RENT	RENT	RENT	RENT
TAXES	TAXES	TAXES	TAXES
CLEANING FEES	CLEANING FEES	CLEANING FEES	CLEANING FEES

Date ________________

DATE ________________	DATE ________________	DATE ________________	DATE ________________
Renter Information			
Name			
Address			
City, State, Zip			
Telephone			
E-Mail			
# of Nights			
______ Adults ______ Children			
# of Vehicles			
Tag #			
Pets			
Referral Site			
Date Reserved			
Rate			
Fees			
Taxes			
Check List			
Sent Billing Agreement ❐	❐	❐	❐
Rental Rules ❐	❐	❐	❐
Directions ❐	❐	❐	❐
Deposit Returned ❐	❐	❐	❐
Rec. Deposit & Signed Rules ❐	❐	❐	❐
1st Payment ❐	❐	❐	❐
2nd Payment ❐	❐	❐	❐
Scheduled Cleaning ❐	❐	❐	❐
Cleaning Feedback ❐	❐	❐	❐
WEEKLY TOTALS	**NIGHTLY TOTALS**	**NIGHTLY TOTALS**	**NIGHTLY TOTALS**
RENT	**RENT**	**RENT**	**RENT**
TAXES	**TAXES**	**TAXES**	**TAXES**
CLEANING FEES	**CLEANING FEES**	**CLEANING FEES**	**CLEANING FEES**

Date ____________________

DATE ____________	DATE ____________	DATE ____________	DATE ____________
❐	❐	❐	❐
❐	❐	❐	❐
❐	❐	❐	❐
❐	❐	❐	❐
❐	❐	❐	❐
❐	❐	❐	❐
❐	❐	❐	❐
❐	❐	❐	❐
❐	❐	❐	❐
NIGHTLY TOTALS	NIGHTLY TOTALS	NIGHTLY TOTALS	NIGHTLY TOTALS
RENT	RENT	RENT	RENT
TAXES	TAXES	TAXES	TAXES
CLEANING FEES	CLEANING FEES	CLEANING FEES	CLEANING FEES

Date ____________

DATE____________	DATE____________	DATE____________	DATE____________
Renter Information			
Name			
Address			
City, State, Zip			
Telephone			
E-Mail			
# of Nights			
______ Adults ______ Children			
# of Vehicles			
Tag #			
Pets			
Referral Site			
Date Reserved			
Rate			
Fees			
Taxes			
Check List			
Sent Billing Agreement ❐	❐	❐	❐
Rental Rules ❐	❐	❐	❐
Directions ❐	❐	❐	❐
Deposit Returned ❐	❐	❐	❐
Rec. Deposit & Signed Rules ❐	❐	❐	❐
1st Payment ❐	❐	❐	❐
2nd Payment ❐	❐	❐	❐
Scheduled Cleaning ❐	❐	❐	❐
Cleaning Feedback ❐	❐	❐	❐
WEEKLY TOTALS	**NIGHTLY TOTALS**	**NIGHTLY TOTALS**	**NIGHTLY TOTALS**
RENT	**RENT**	**RENT**	**RENT**
TAXES	**TAXES**	**TAXES**	**TAXES**
CLEANING FEES	**CLEANING FEES**	**CLEANING FEES**	**CLEANING FEES**

Date ____________

DATE ____________	DATE ____________	DATE ____________	DATE ____________
❐	❐	❐	❐
❐	❐	❐	❐
❐	❐	❐	❐
❐	❐	❐	❐
❐	❐	❐	❐
❐	❐	❐	❐
❐	❐	❐	❐
❐	❐	❐	❐
❐	❐	❐	❐
NIGHTLY TOTALS	NIGHTLY TOTALS	NIGHTLY TOTALS	NIGHTLY TOTALS
RENT	RENT	RENT	RENT
TAXES	TAXES	TAXES	TAXES
CLEANING FEES	CLEANING FEES	CLEANING FEES	CLEANING FEES

Date ____________________

DATE____________	DATE____________	DATE____________	DATE____________
Renter Information			
Name			
Address			
City, State, Zip			
Telephone			
E-Mail			
# of Nights			
______ Adults ______ Children			
# of Vehicles			
Tag #			
Pets			
Referral Site			
Date Reserved			
Rate			
Fees			
Taxes			
Check List			
Sent Billing Agreement ❐	❐	❐	❐
Rental Rules ❐	❐	❐	❐
Directions ❐	❐	❐	❐
Deposit Returned ❐	❐	❐	❐
Rec. Deposit & Signed Rules ❐	❐	❐	❐
1st Payment ❐	❐	❐	❐
2nd Payment ❐	❐	❐	❐
Scheduled Cleaning ❐	❐	❐	❐
Cleaning Feedback ❐	❐	❐	❐
WEEKLY TOTALS	**NIGHTLY TOTALS**	**NIGHTLY TOTALS**	**NIGHTLY TOTALS**
RENT	**RENT**	**RENT**	**RENT**
TAXES	**TAXES**	**TAXES**	**TAXES**
CLEANING FEES	**CLEANING FEES**	**CLEANING FEES**	**CLEANING FEES**

Date ____________

DATE ____________	DATE ____________	DATE ____________	DATE ____________
❐	❐	❐	❐
❐	❐	❐	❐
❐	❐	❐	❐
❐	❐	❐	❐
❐	❐	❐	❐
❐	❐	❐	❐
❐	❐	❐	❐
❐	❐	❐	❐
❐	❐	❐	❐
NIGHTLY TOTALS	NIGHTLY TOTALS	NIGHTLY TOTALS	NIGHTLY TOTALS
RENT	RENT	RENT	RENT
TAXES	TAXES	TAXES	TAXES
CLEANING FEES	CLEANING FEES	CLEANING FEES	CLEANING FEES

Income

DATE	GUEST	RENTAL DATES	CHECK#/CONF#	AMOUNT
12 Feb. 04	Smith	March 27-April 1	Ck #2345	$200.00
12 Feb. 04	Jones	September 4-11	Paypal 0123456-7	$915.23

YEAR ______ TOTAL ______

Income

DATE	GUEST	RENTAL DATES	CHECK#/CONF#	AMOUNT
12 Feb. 04	Smith	March 27-April 1	Ck #2345	$200.00
12 Feb. 04	Jones	September 4-11	Paypal 0123456-7	$915.23

YEAR

TOTAL

Income

DATE	GUEST	RENTAL DATES	CHECK#/CONF#	AMOUNT
12 Feb. 04	Smith	March 27-April 1	Ck #2345	$200.00
12 Feb. 04	Jones	September 4-11	Paypal 0123456-7	$915.23

YEAR

TOTAL

Income

DATE	GUEST	RENTAL DATES	CHECK#/CONF#	AMOUNT
12 Feb. 04	Smith	March 27-April 1	Ck #2345	$200.00
12 Feb. 04	Jones	September 4-11	Paypal 0123456-7	$915.23

YEAR

TOTAL

Income

DATE	GUEST	RENTAL DATES	CHECK#/CONF#	AMOUNT
12 Feb. 04	Smith	March 27-April 1	Ck #2345	$200.00
12 Feb. 04	Jones	September 4-11	Paypal 0123456-7	$915:23

YEAR ______ TOTAL ______

DATE	GUEST	RENTAL DATES	CHECK#/CONF#	AMOUNT
12 Feb. 04	Smith	March 27-April 1	Ck #2345	$200.00
12 Feb. 04	Jones	September 4-11	Paypal 0123456-7	$915.23

YEAR ______ TOTAL ______

Expenses

DATE	VENDOR	DESCRIPTION	CHECK#/CONF#	AMOUNT
19 Oct. 04	Walmart	Pillow Cases	Ck #1023	$21.84
01 Nov. 03	Phone	Regular Bill	AMEX payment	$24.91
	Final Cost to Tony			
	Furniture			
	Supplies			
	Appliances			
1-31-14	City PF W&S	water to build	31.29 online	31.29
2-10-14	Amazon	Vac. Rental Organizer	26.04	26.04
	Home Depot	windows & Doors	VISA	9139.57
	"	Cabinets-Kitchen	VISA	1642.63

	YEAR		TOTAL	

Expenses

DATE	VENDOR	DESCRIPTION	CHECK#/CONF#	AMOUNT
19 Oct. 04	Walmart	Pillow Cases	Ck #1023	$21.84
01 Nov. 03	Phone	Regular Bill	AMEX payment	$24.91

YEAR

TOTAL

Expenses

DATE	VENDOR	DESCRIPTION	CHECK#/CONF#	AMOUNT
19 Oct. 04	Walmart	Pillow Cases	Ck #1023	$21.84
01 Nov. 03	Phone	Regular Bill	AMEX payment	$24.91

YEAR

TOTAL

Expenses

DATE	VENDOR	DESCRIPTION	CHECK#/CONF#	AMOUNT
19 Oct. 04	Walmart	Pillow Cases	Ck #1023	$21.84
01 Nov. 03	Phone	Regular Bill	AMEX payment	$24.91

YEAR ______ TOTAL ______

Expenses

DATE	VENDOR	DESCRIPTION	CHECK#/CONF#	AMOUNT
19 Oct. 04	Walmart	Pillow Cases	Ck #1023	$21.84
01 Nov. 03	Phone	Regular Bill	AMEX payment	$24.91

YEAR

TOTAL

Expenses

DATE	VENDOR	DESCRIPTION	CHECK#/CONF#	AMOUNT
19 Oct. 04	Walmart	Pillow Cases	Ck #1023	$21.84
01 Nov. 03	Phone	Regular Bill	AMEX payment	$24.91

YEAR

TOTAL

Notes

DATE	NOTES
10/3	Bring laundry detergent and light bulbs next time.

DATE	NOTES
10/3	Bring laundry detergent and light bulbs next time.

Notes

DATE	NOTES
10/3	Bring laundry detergent and light bulbs next time.

2009

January

S	M	T	W	T	F	S
				1	2	3
4	5	6	7	8	9	10
11	12	13	14	15	16	17
18	19	20	21	22	23	24
25	26	27	28	29	30	31

February

S	M	T	W	T	F	S
1	2	3	4	5	6	7
8	9	10	11	12	13	14
15	16	17	18	19	20	21
22	23	24	25	26	27	28

March

S	M	T	W	T	F	S
1	2	3	4	5	6	7
8	9	10	11	12	13	14
15	16	17	18	19	20	21
22	23	24	25	26	27	28
29	30	31				

April

S	M	T	W	T	F	S
			1	2	3	4
5	6	7	8	9	10	11
12	13	14	15	16	17	18
19	20	21	22	23	24	25
26	27	28	29	30		

May

S	M	T	W	T	F	S
					1	2
3	4	5	6	7	8	9
10	11	12	13	14	15	16
17	18	19	20	21	22	23
24	25	26	27	28	29	30
31						

June

S	M	T	W	T	F	S
	1	2	3	4	5	6
7	8	9	10	11	12	13
14	15	16	17	18	19	20
21	22	23	24	25	26	27
28	29	30				

July

S	M	T	W	T	F	S
			1	2	3	4
5	6	7	8	9	10	11
12	13	14	15	16	17	18
19	20	21	22	23	24	25
26	27	28	29	30	31	

August

S	M	T	W	T	F	S
						1
2	3	4	5	6	7	8
9	10	11	12	13	14	15
16	17	18	19	20	21	22
23	24	25	26	27	28	29
30	31					

September

S	M	T	W	T	F	S
		1	2	3	4	5
6	7	8	9	10	11	12
13	14	15	16	17	18	19
20	21	22	23	24	25	26
27	28	29	30			

October

S	M	T	W	T	F	S
				1	2	3
4	5	6	7	8	9	10
11	12	13	14	15	16	17
18	19	20	21	22	23	24
25	26	27	28	29	30	31

November

S	M	T	W	T	F	S
1	2	3	4	5	6	7
8	9	10	11	12	13	14
15	16	17	18	19	20	21
22	23	24	25	26	27	28
29	30					

December

S	M	T	W	T	F	S
		1	2	3	4	5
6	7	8	9	10	11	12
13	14	15	16	17	18	19
20	21	22	23	24	25	26
27	28	29	30	31		

2010

January

S	M	T	W	T	F	S
					1	2
3	4	5	6	7	8	9
10	11	12	13	14	15	16
17	18	19	20	21	22	23
24	25	26	27	28	29	30
31						

February

S	M	T	W	T	F	S
	1	2	3	4	5	6
7	8	9	10	11	12	13
14	15	16	17	18	19	20
21	22	23	24	25	26	27
28						

March

S	M	T	W	T	F	S
	1	2	3	4	5	6
7	8	9	10	11	12	13
14	15	16	17	18	19	20
21	22	23	24	25	26	27
28	29	30	31			

April

S	M	T	W	T	F	S
				1	2	3
4	5	6	7	8	9	10
11	12	13	14	15	16	17
18	19	20	21	22	23	24
25	26	27	28	29	30	

May

S	M	T	W	T	F	S
						1
2	3	4	5	6	7	8
9	10	11	12	13	14	15
16	17	18	19	20	21	22
23	24	25	26	27	28	29
30	31					

June

S	M	T	W	T	F	S
		1	2	3	4	5
6	7	8	9	10	11	12
13	14	15	16	17	18	19
20	21	22	23	24	25	26
27	28	29	30			

July

S	M	T	W	T	F	S
				1	2	3
4	5	6	7	8	9	10
11	12	13	14	15	16	17
18	19	20	21	22	23	24
25	26	27	28	29	30	31

August

S	M	T	W	T	F	S
1	2	3	4	5	6	7
8	9	10	11	12	13	14
15	16	17	18	19	20	21
22	23	24	25	26	27	28
29	30	31				

September

S	M	T	W	T	F	S
			1	2	3	4
5	6	7	8	9	10	11
12	13	14	15	16	17	18
19	20	21	22	23	24	25
26	27	28	29	30		

October

S	M	T	W	T	F	S
					1	2
3	4	5	6	7	8	9
10	11	12	13	14	15	16
17	18	19	20	21	22	23
24	25	26	27	28	29	30
31						

November

S	M	T	W	T	F	S
	1	2	3	4	5	6
7	8	9	10	11	12	13
14	15	16	17	18	19	20
21	22	23	24	25	26	27
28	29	30				

December

S	M	T	W	T	F	S
			1	2	3	4
5	6	7	8	9	10	11
12	13	14	15	16	17	18
19	20	21	22	23	24	25
26	27	28	29	30	31	

2011

January

S	M	T	W	T	F	S
						1
2	3	4	5	6	7	8
9	10	11	12	13	14	15
16	17	18	19	20	21	22
23	24	25	26	27	28	29
30	31					

February

S	M	T	W	T	F	S
		1	2	3	4	5
6	7	8	9	10	11	12
13	14	15	16	17	18	19
20	21	22	23	24	25	26
27	28					

March

S	M	T	W	T	F	S
		1	2	3	4	5
6	7	8	9	10	11	12
13	14	15	16	17	18	19
20	21	22	23	24	25	26
27	28	29	30	31		

April

S	M	T	W	T	F	S
					1	2
3	4	5	6	7	8	9
10	11	12	13	14	15	16
17	18	19	20	21	22	23
24	25	26	27	28	29	30

May

S	M	T	W	T	F	S
1	2	3	4	5	6	7
8	9	10	11	12	13	14
15	16	17	18	19	20	21
22	23	24	25	26	27	28
29	30	31				

June

S	M	T	W	T	F	S
			1	2	3	4
5	6	7	8	9	10	11
12	13	14	15	16	17	18
19	20	21	22	23	24	25
26	27	28	29	30		

July

S	M	T	W	T	F	S
					1	2
3	4	5	6	7	8	9
10	11	12	13	14	15	16
17	18	19	20	21	22	23
24	25	26	27	28	29	30
31						

August

S	M	T	W	T	F	S
	1	2	3	4	5	6
7	8	9	10	11	12	13
14	15	16	17	18	19	20
21	22	23	24	25	26	27
28	29	30	31			

September

S	M	T	W	T	F	S
				1	2	3
4	5	6	7	8	9	10
11	12	13	14	15	16	17
18	19	20	21	22	23	24
25	26	27	28	29	30	

October

S	M	T	W	T	F	S
						1
2	3	4	5	6	7	8
9	10	11	12	13	14	15
16	17	18	19	20	21	22
23	24	25	26	27	28	29
30	31					

November

S	M	T	W	T	F	S
		1	2	3	4	5
6	7	8	9	10	11	12
13	14	15	16	17	18	19
20	21	22	23	24	25	26
27	28	29	30			

December

S	M	T	W	T	F	S
				1	2	3
4	5	6	7	8	9	10
11	12	13	14	15	16	17
18	19	20	21	22	23	24
25	26	27	28	29	30	31

Holidays circled

Order Form

Online Orders: www.HowToRentByOwner.com

Fax Orders: 530–654–8235

E-mail Orders: orders@HowToRentByOwner.com

Name

Address

City, State, Zip

Telephone

Email

Web Site Address

Shipping:

US: Add $5 for first product and $3 for each additional product.

International: $ 10 for first product and $6 for each additional product.

Payment:

❒ Visa ❒ MasterCard

___________ Amount

Card Number Exp. Date

Name on card

Address where bills sent

Products:

How to Rent Vacation Properties By Owner	$26 Book	Quantity_________
The Vacation Rental Organizer	$19 Book	Quantity_________
The Essentials of Owning and Renting Vacation Properties	$39 DVD	Quantity_________